I'D RATHER KILL MYSELF THAN BE A LAWYER

HOW ANYONE CAN FIND HAPPINESS

Robert Segall, JD

D1361481

ROBERT SEGALL, JD

Book Layout © 2020 Daydreamz Publishing
Cover Layout © 2020 Sonia Naz

I'd Rather Kill Myself Than Be a Lawyer/ Robert Segall, JD. -- 1st ed.

Dedication

This book is dedicated to the millions of people "looking for happiness."

Happiness is kind of like bacteria. It lives inside of us from the day we are born. Sometimes it grows. Sometimes it protects us. Sometimes, when ignored, it causes irritable bowel syndrome.

My suggestion is to scrape the crap off your happiness and let it breathe. Be kind to yourself.

And remember to always to tell the people you love, including yourself, every day:

Thank you.
I'm sorry.
I love you, and...
I don't give a shit (even when you are talking to yourself).

"Have a happy day."
-Audrey Segall

Dad's favorite picture of me. New City, New York. Circa 1972

**"Death is the solution to all problems.
No man — no problem."**

-Joseph Stalin

**"Hello world, here's a song that we're singing,
come on get happy..."**

-The Partridge Family

Table of Contents

**"To be or not to be.
That's not really a question."**

—Jean-Luc Godard

The world was fading away. My eyes froze on the plain, off-white walls of my small associate's office. There I sat at age 29, thirty-two floors up at 230 Park Avenue in the mid-town Manhattan law office of Ohrenstein and Brown where I was employed as an associate. I was paralyzed by a combination of overwhelming fear and overwhelming drowsiness.

I saw the words on my law school diploma, black and white, the letters a testament to an unwanted accomplishment. I should have used it to wipe my ass when it was handed to me instead of hanging it on the wall as a reminder of my last seven and half years of misery. That fucking diploma was going to outlive me.

Next to me sat a pill bottle recently emptied down my throat.

Oh shit, I thought, as everything started to get blurry. *This is happening. I'm dying.*

At that moment, I did what any self-respecting, despondent, suicidal, nice Jewish boy would do…

I called my mother.

"Hello?"

"Mom…?"

"Hi, Robbie. What's up?"

Good news/bad news, I thought. *The good news is I'll be moving closer to you. The bad news is I'll be in the cemetery.*

"Mom, you or Dad may want to call someone right now. I'm at my office and I need to get to the hospital."

I remember that moment. Her panic. Her fear. Then everything went dark as I faded away.

I didn't understand it at the time, but I wasn't just ending my pain — I was punishing my parents. My subconscious mind whispered that my mom and dad, who'd expected too much from me, who'd insisted on law school, had caused this to happen. And now, like in some action movie, they had just minutes to save my life. *Take that, fuckers.*

I now know all they were guilty of was loving me.

Mom fixing my hair. Circa 1973, New City, New York.
I think she over-brushed it. It all fell out.

Looking back, during all of the therapy and discussion, I never actually fully regretted the suicide attempt. In my mind, it somehow saved me.

Of course, I could also just have quit my job. That probably would have been easier.

My bad.

I started and stopped writing a book about finding happiness approximately twenty times over the past eight years.

I wasn't certain if it was my lack of ability, impatience or lack of confidence, but I was getting nowhere. I kept trying and kept quitting.

The most frustrating part was not being able to simply put it to rest, just to accept the fact that I would never finish the book.

Yet, after each failed effort, sometimes after weeks and sometimes after months, I was inevitably drawn back to my computer. I couldn't escape the compulsion to tell the story of how I rebuilt my life after a suicide attempt in my late 20s to become a (better) husband, father, businessperson, and community member, and most importantly, how I found happiness so many years later.

Then I would quit writing again.

Much self-reflection guided me to the conclusion that I kept failing for the following reasons:

- *Reason 1*: I was not a good writer.

- *Reason 2:* I was full of shit. I had not found happiness.

Reason 1. I can string two interesting and occasionally humorous ideas together, but a book? I felt I possessed neither the organizational skill nor the grasp of sentence structure needed for such a weighty endeavor. At one point, I even hired a ghostwriter. She took the several hundred pages of crap I'd composed and pulled together a much more cogent and organized...piece of crap.

It was certainly not her fault. I had not provided the necessary content to make the book readable. Her writing was strong, but the voice was not mine.

All of this led me to the conclusion that as excruciating as a suicidal depression can be, writing about it *really* made me want to kill myself.

Now I know that last statement might make some of you cringe. You may be thinking, "How dare you compare writing a book to depression?"

"You are insensitive. This is serious stuff. How can you make light of it?"

And the all-time most cringe-worthy statement, "You are making me uncomfortable!"

To you, I lovingly say, "Relax Snowflake."

This is my book and that was a joke. That is one of the important themes in life. There are times in life where if we don't laugh, we will cry.

And it was one major reason I kept trying to write the book. I am pretty good at being funny, so I understand laughing can take us out of some serious mental garbage. My belief has been that if I can help someone being crushed by their brain by injecting some laughter (and hopefully useable advice), isn't it cool, and kind of my responsibility to try?

Thus, I kept at it, anxiously awaiting the day I would unveil my authorship to the world. Or at least to my friends and family, who will hopefully placate me by reading it.

Reason 2. With respect to my being full of shit, it turns out my lack of writing ability was only 97% of the problem.

The important other 3% was that I was unqualified to write about happiness. I knew plenty about looking for happiness, but so not much about finding it. I was not happy, so writing a book about finding happiness made no sense. Again, I was full of shit.

This book needed a happy ending.[1]

What Changed

In his groundbreaking book *The Power of Now*, Eckhardt Tolle declares that,

> *If you find your here and now intolerable and it makes you unhappy, you have three options:*

---

[1] Pun intended.

> *remove yourself from the situation, **change it** or **accept** it totally. If you want to take responsibility for your life, you must choose one of those three options, and you must choose now.*

I love Eckhardt Tolle and especially *The Power of Now.* I found the message of being present to be transformative. I found the quote above particularly powerful. Yet, even after reading the book multiple times and internalizing it, I still struggled to consistently apply that particular principle as it related to happiness.

Thinking about the book and that particular passage for quite a while, it finally occurred to me why his excellent advice was not penetrating my somewhat oversized skull. As it related to me, I felt it needed one more piece to be complete. It was this:

> *If you choose to change, you must **believe** you can change. And you must believe **now**.*

With apologies to Mr. Tolle, who I am certain presumed *belief* was part of the equation, as much as I wanted to change, I didn't believe I could be consistently happy. I felt it was not in my DNA.

I had experienced many happy moments in my life. For example, the first time I had sex. And the second time, because it proved the first time wasn't an accident. Also, my wedding day, the birth of our children, and that one time recently I was able to sleep through the night without being awakened four or five times to pee.

Nonetheless, even with many happy individual moments, I was never truly, *consistently* happy.

I lacked the ability to properly deal with the stresses of life. The reasons and the coping mechanisms I tried are the basis of this book.

My particular issues usually originated from work or work-related events, and before that from school. Given that I've been working or in school 90% of my life, I have been stressed for approximately 47 years.

The routine never changed. Each day I woke up and was welcomed by the cold embrace of paralyzing stress, anxiety, and fear. As each day progressed, I would work my way out of it. By the end of the day, I felt better, went home, saw my family, did something enjoyable or fun, and went to sleep, just to wake up to the same shit all over again the next day.

On a few rare special days, stress invited its friend depression over to say hello. Those days turned into weeks or months. You cannot work your way out of depression over the course of the day the way you may be able to with stress.

I suppose I was thankful that stress, not depression, was my main problem. Stress seemed a bit easier to control, at least temporarily. Stress or depression. A real *Sophie's Choice* of mental problems.

For me, anxiety meant something was always setting me off or making me feel *less than*, or I was waiting for that *one thing* to happen, such as a client taking the action I recommended or something good happening for my kids. All of those things caused me anxiety to the point where I never fully enjoyed anything.

My entire life, I **accepted** this situation. I assumed this was my lot in life. Despite working diligently for twenty-three years to accept enjoyment and happiness, I never reached "HAPPY."

And I accepted that as my reality.

Until I couldn't anymore.

After more than five decades living in this personal hell, I reached my tipping point. At that moment I finally knew I could *change* it because I had no other choice. I could no longer accept the status quo. My choices were either believe I could consistently be happy or jump off a fucking bridge, which was never an option. The nearest bridge around here isn't high enough.

In late 2017/early 2018, following another successful but very stressful work year, a ridiculous, unimportant, inconsequential issue got me so unhinged it almost caused a mini breakdown. I purposely don't mention the actual triggering event because it doesn't matter. There was always something upsetting me. It was nothing different or exceptional this time around.

What *was* different this time was that when I reached my breaking point, something snapped (or better put, *clicked*) and instead of breaking, I bent. I told myself, *That's enough. I don't want to feel this way anymore. Any one of us could be dead tomorrow and none of this shit would matter.*

I was fed up. I had this great life with family and friends, a successful career and I was sick and fucking tired of being miserable. I'd had enough. I needed to change something.

At that moment, I was forced to **believe** change was possible because I could not live with the constant daily struggles. I was fed up and, unlike when I was in my twenties, punching my ticket out of life didn't cross my mind.

I rededicated myself to revisiting all of my work toward wellness over the past 23 or so years and making it my number one priority. It was then things started to gel.

Of course, had it been as easy as deciding I'd had enough and moving on, this wouldn't be much of a book. Being fed up was the easy part.

What came after — my willingness to actually pay attention to and apply what I had learned, and discuss what I discovered and how it helped set me on the road to ongoing happiness — was the difficult part.

Much of the difficulty was rooted in embarrassment as I acknowledged one of the primary byproducts of not being happy:

My big mouth.

As you may have already deduced, I am pretty candid with my thoughts and I think I am funny. I think the title of this book captures both of those traits.

What the title does not capture is the fact that my candor was often unkind. My mind was fueled by the anger that arose from not being happy. It caused me to say and do stupid shit that created problems for me throughout my life. I would say anything, irrespective of the situation. That in turn would piss off people and alienate them, causing me further unhappiness.

My nonstop commentary created myriad embarrassing and problematic interactions that slowed my progress in many aspects of my life.

Why couldn't I stop talking?

Why were my words so cutting?

Because I wasn't happy.

Wait.

Didn't I just say I wasn't happy because I had a big mouth? Now I am saying I had a big mouth because I wasn't happy? Which one was it?

Actually, they happened together. At a young age I was taught:

    a. Stress as a default
    b. Humor/candor as a defense mechanism

These were inter-related and began early in my life.

Further complicating matters was that my mind/mouth could also be an asset, so simply turning them off was not the right option. Not everything I said, even poorly timed, had a negative impact. It is often challenging to find humor in tough situations. My lack of filter has been a plus in some difficult times. The right words can lighten a mood by shedding light on how unimportant most things really are.

Take for example, my suicide attempt. At the lowest point in my life, when I was not thinking clearly, *I literally decided it would better to be dead than spend another day practicing law.*

Come on. That shit is funny.

Why Pick on Lawyers?

This book has almost nothing to do with lawyers. The entire idea for a book actually came from the title, which popped into my head several years ago while I considered the events of April 12, 1995, the day I tried to kill myself. I thought the title was really funny and wanted to build a joke around it. I started writing the joke eight years ago and didn't stop. Now I have a book.

To be clear, I don't particularly like lawyers. I never did. As a species I find them to be mostly egotistical, stressed out, miserable, angry douche canoes.

This is ironic given that so many people in my family practice or practiced law — my wife Karin, both my brothers Mo and Steve, my brother-in-law, Ken, my cousin

Corey, his father (my uncle Gil) who was a judge most of his career, my uncle Kenny and many other relatives.

For the most part, my family was not the reason I felt this way. I also understand the need for lawyers - they protect artists' rights, make sure we are not taken advantage of when we purchase property or sign a contract, fight for our civil rights, etc.

They seem necessary in a civilized society.

My main issue with lawyers is that the profession attracts a disproportionate number of assholes. I saw this during law school as I dealt with insufferable, competitive dickheads and arrogant professors. This was followed by my brief four and a half years of practice, where many of the people I encountered at work were nasty, unhappy assholes. Not all of them, but a disproportionately large number. Finally, I had interactions with lawyers post-law-career, which only strengthened my belief that lawyers are yucky.

My second issue is they work in a profession where blame is their number one product. I address that in the chapter on accountability.

Thus concludes most of the lawyer bashing I will do in this book. I'll save the rest for my next book, tentatively entitled *Lawyers Suck Ass*.

Anyway, if you purchased this book hoping it was all about lawyer bashing, sorry to disappoint you. We are in solidarity in disliking lawyers, but that is for another day.

> **"Books serve to show a man**
> **that those original thoughts of his**
> **aren't very new after all."**
> —*Abraham Lincoln*

The very first step in uncovering happiness is recognizing that in most cases, whatever you are suffering is normal.

I walked through much of my life believing the opposite and therefore thought my problems were unfixable.

I Am Very Interesting

My initial reason for writing a book was to talk about life lessons I learned post-overdose.

For the better part of twenty-five years, I've spent time with mentors and coaches, in therapy and in self-reflection, all the while habitually keeping journals filled with "lessons learned." I made notes of discussions on attachment, to outcome, happiness, fear, love, and countless other wellness-themed ideas designed to reduce my always elevated anxiety levels.

The premise of the book was to explain how I applied those lessons to achieve happiness post-breakdown. I imagined that describing my journey would be a great read and helpful to others, as my situation was unique. My road to happiness was compelling and my problems were particularly interesting.

Embarking on my writing journey, I thought the only potential problem would be how unique my life had been. I believed my story would not be relevant to most people. The challenges I'd encountered were in a category all to themselves.

I Am Not That Interesting

As with all great authors, I conducted research for the book. This included dissecting my time in therapy, analyzing my years working with an excellent spiritual mentor/life/business coach, reading books about happiness and life (including *The Power of Now*, *10% Happier* and *The Art of Happiness)*, and having discussions with family, friends and colleagues on how they've dealt with stress, anxiety and the search for happiness.

My research led me to two conclusions. First, my book may actually be helpful. There are a lot of people dealing with anxiety and stress and battling depression who didn't feel happy. Unfortunately, many of them have considered suicide.

The second conclusion was surprising. My internal struggles weren't special. Not only were they relatable, they were *ordinary*. My stress was no different than anyone else's stress.   The notion that I was unique or special was a self-indulgent clusterfuck.

I just did a really shitty job of handling stuff.

Bad Boy

The things I struggled with, including stress, anxiety, worry, happiness, etc., have always been human challenges. They are not only common in the fastmoving modern world, they have been that way forever. I am certain when shit went down on the prairie or during a joust or in the local cave, our ancestors were pretty fucking stressed.   It is how they reacted that mattered.

Modern reaction to stress is no different, whether it be meditation or breathing or taking a hike. Some folks may take an Ambien or a Prozac to calm down. The only thing unique about my story is that I took the entire fucking bottle, although in fairness it did calm me right down.

To be consistently happy, I needed to acknowledge that the main themes of my life — self-doubt, fear, insecurity, and anxiety — were definitely fixable, but only by me.

This realization was a bit unsettling. It meant being accountable. *Accountability* meant accepting the hard truth that my *issues* were not special. My flaws and anxieties were regular. They were exactly what everyone else was feeling.

"Perhaps," I wondered out loud, "if I could better deal with my internal crap maybe I could consistently be happy."

"No shit," I replied to myself.

It reminded me of the adage, *happiness is possible*. You've probably seen that splashed across those horrible posters where a cat is sitting in a bowl covered in spaghetti. Cats suck but the message is accurate.

The fact remains that happiness actually is possible, and it is up to each individual, not external circumstances, to make it happen.

Owning My Shit

With this newfound knowledge, I pivoted and decided that the book is written about everyone, not just Rob Segall.

This book is for everyone trying to reclaim their brain; anyone who battles the recurrent pulls of anxiety, stress, and depression kicking them in the nuts every day and robbing them of their happiness.

We are all pretty much the same. For much of my life I felt as if the world I wanted, meaning a world where I was happier, was out of my reach. There was a time when I was as far down as anyone can be without being six feet under. I got very close to that point.

Yet even after surviving that, like you, I've still struggled throughout my life to feel good.

To be happy.

That is the truth, folks, and it applies to all of us. When it comes to problems, we are not special despite our parents telling us we are. We all suffer from the same shit. It might smell different, but it is all just crap.

Hard Work Beats Talent When Talent Doesn't Work Hard

This is not a story of failure or of lives wasted. I used the plural there because had I been successful in taking my life, my three amazing kids would have died with me. Forgetting the unthinkable toll my suicide would have taken on Karin (that attempt was hard enough on her), I get sick thinking about our kids. I am forever grateful I failed that day.

While my problems and general personality flaws are not particularly unique, I believe my resolve to change them was greater than average. Change is not free. That is also what this book is about.

My story is not sunshine, unicorns, and rainbows flying out of my ass. My brain and my mouth made life much more challenging than it needed to be. Fighting through that complicated maze has always been difficult. Almost impossible. That is why it took so long to complete this book. It could be only be written as a success story, so for most of my life it could not be written.

I have put in a shitload of work on myself and continue to do so every day. If you don't put in the work to own your flaws and address them, you will continue being weighed down by them. Mine is a comeback story, but it applies to anyone who does the work to feel better and improve his/her life.

I tried many of the coping mechanisms available in the civilized world. I found that you can drink herbal tea, meditate, study the Talmud, chant, practice tai chi or engage in any of the other mental gymnastics to which we subject ourselves and still struggle to find psychic relief.

All of those things are excellent practices to control your temperament and lower your pulse and will move you toward becoming a happier person. None of it matters, however, if you don't learn that the driver of happiness is *how you think*.

If you're like me and struggle every day against your thoughts, you have to put in the work to make the change you want to see. Otherwise, you are just spinning your wheels.

Albert Einstein said, "The definition of insanity is doing the same thing over and over again and expecting different results."

Stop being insane. Try being happy.

"Don't try suicide.
You're just gonna hate it."

-Queen

L est there be any confusion, this is not a book about suicide.

I am not a trained mental health professional. Everything you read here is based on my own personal experience or observations. That includes my own brush with death, people with whom I had a personal connection who killed themselves, others I know who tried to end it, and a lifetime of dealing with extreme anxiety and a few isolated but significant bouts with depression.

I'm not qualified to tell you what medicine to take or doctor to visit, or to pursue holistic remedies. None of it. Nothing I discuss is meant to include people with terminal illness, people living in severe, incurable pain or people with ongoing severe psychological issues. I am not qualified to address that population and it would be irresponsible to offer an opinion if I had one.

I am only qualified to share my personal experience regarding suicide.

My Philosophy on Suicide

Suicide is a really, really, really, *really* bad idea.

Had I been good at suicide, I would have missed some pretty cool stuff in my life. Stuff I didn't know I was capable of achieving. I also would have missed out on loving my wife, three awesome kids, great friends, a great job…

A great life.

Remember that while all those cool things *felt* a million miles away when I was in my deep depression, they were right next to me. I was just blind to everything but the negatives. While you might feel as if everything you look at is dark, there is a good chance you are actually right next to the light.

How Suicide Feels

If you have reached the point of suicidal thoughts or are contemplating it or planning to act because of prolonged, severe distress, this may sound familiar:

> 1.) **Loneliness-** You are either afraid to tell people you are depressed and/or suicidal, or the people you told don't understand the gravity of your feelings. You feel alone.

2.) **No other option-** You believe you have no other option.

If this is where you are, you need to do two things:

1) *Take yourself seriously.* Immediately speak to your family, your doctor, a counselor, or a mental health professional. There is nothing more important than asking for help from the right source because *you cannot help yourself.* That is like trying to solve the problem with the problem — your brain.

You are never alone.

2) Above all else, remember *death is not an option.* You always have other options. You are just too weighted down to see them.

Real Sickness

One of the many horrible parts about psychological challenges is that people think you are full of shit or that you can simply "snap out of it" when you say you suffer from depression or anxiety.

"Smile," "Suck it up," "You have a good life," or "Everybody gets stressed", are some of the gems I've heard over and over through the years. You hear that enough times and you start to believe you are defective because everyone else seems to be able to let their problems roll off them. That, by the way, is bullshit. They may not show it, but everyone struggles in one way or another.

Imagine if you called your friend with the flu and told him to "snap out of it." How about a relative with cancer? Why not say to them, "It's all good, bro. You'll shake this."

Really? How about this? How about, "Go fuck yourself"?

People feel they can talk you out of your psychological sickness. With mental illness, everyone thinks that's acceptable, because your brain is not in a cast or a sling.

Then, to make matters worse, when a person has a breakdown or, in the most extreme example, commits suicide, people react with "I didn't know," or "They seemed fine."

We have been conditioned to view mental health this way, which is why people are reluctant to talk about it. While I am open today about my experience, for years afterward I was ashamed and embarrassed to discuss what had happened. I know being viewed in that light has impacted the speed at which I move to have this book published.

Loneliness

In 1995, no one knew quite how bad I felt. They knew I felt pretty fucking bad, but no one imagined I was going to try to kill myself.

I suppose that is the reality of many suicides and suicide attempts. People shy away from contemplating their own death, so the idea that someone we know might try to hasten their own death is not usually considered by non-depressed people.

As a result, depression and the moment leading up to suicide feel very lonely. You feel as if you are all by yourself in your pain.

The irony was that I was not alone at all. I had my wife Karin and several other family and friends whom I could have told. Even though telling them I wanted to die would have been beyond difficult, it would have been far easier than the shit I eventually made them (and me) experience.

Options

Another horrible part about psychological issues is feeling as if you have a complete lack of options.

The moment before I took those pills, that was exactly what I thought. I believed I had no other choice.

Somehow, in my cluttered mind, **I convinced myself that being a lawyer, something *I never wanted to do it the first place*, was the *only* thing I could do.**

In fact, my other choices, aside from killing myself, were *literally anything else I wanted to try!* I could have just quit law and gotten a job flipping burgers or selling vacuum cleaners or washing windows or tried for a job on Wall Street and they all would have been better than being dead.

The irony is that I actually did end up doing many other things which worked out. I went from practicing law to working in a warehouse to co-owning a video store to selling financial products to financial advising. I could have skipped the overdose and had the exact same results.

My depressed thoughts twisted everything. I convinced myself that death was better than disappointing my parents, not wanting to be considered a failure or not having money. Worst of all was my most irrational fear, which was that I would disappoint Karin. She would have — and has — loved me through everything, and I *simply did not see it.* My thought process was completely compromised.

To understand choice is to understand the ridiculousness of suicide. There are literally one billion other, better choices than killing yourself. I understand that when you are suicidal you see no other choice than your death, but just think about it. That notion is really fucking silly.

What are some reasons a person might consider suicide? They may include:

- shame
- financial hardship
- breaking up
- loss of a loved one
- bullying
- sickness
- failure in school

These are all really shitty things. And you can add most anything you want to the list.

But is the solution really DEATH?!?!?!!? That is like setting your house on fire because the toilet is clogged.

You are choosing a permanent solution to a temporary problem.

Not too long ago, the notion of the permanence of death (and thus the silliness of suicide) crystalized for me while listening an interview of esteemed journalist Dan Rather by my hero, the King of All Media, Howard Stern. Howard asked him why, in his 80s, Mr. Rather worked as hard as he did. Mr. Rather answered,

"Because when I die, I'll be dead a long time."

That leads me to this chapter's lesson:

If you are considering suicide, you have lost the ability to have rational thought. It is that simple. If you commit suicide, you are being killed by a temporarily insane person.

Remember, on the other side, there is no choice. You are dead.

Why choose *no choice*?

The Suicide Prevention Lifeline provides 24/7, free, and confidential support for people in distress, prevention, and crisis resources for you or your loved ones.

1-800-273-8255

MY STORY

I was an ordinary person with an active life, a loving family and much for which to be grateful. One day I woke up and crossed a line that can never be erased.

I swallowed a bottle of pills in a desperate attempt to end my life. By some miracle I lived and came back, which was an unexpected PLOT TWIST!

This is how and why it happened.

George's Bar Mitzvah, White Plains, New York. April 13, 2019.
That's Molly on my left, George, Pam and Karin. One of many milestones that almost never happened.

**"And you may tell yourself,
this is not my beautiful wife.
And you may tell yourself,
this is not my beautiful house.
And you may ask yourself, how did I get here?"**
-Once in a Lifetime, Talking Heads

April 12, 1995, the day after my overdose. I sat on the 7th floor of NYU Hospital behind the locked doors of the psychiatric unit wondering how the hell my life had ended up this way. Assessing my situation, I thought,

"I am smart."

"I work hard."

"I am pretty fucking funny."

"I am motivated."

I had done every goddamned thing asked of me in my life and achieved what was expected of me. How had I ended up in the hospital? What else was I supposed to do? Why had I taken all those pills?

What a good boy. Bar Mitzvah.
Dellwood Country Club, New City, New York. March 31, 1979.

That was the big question. *Why the hell did I take all those pills?*

Why would a 'normal' person, short of a terminally ill person in severe pain, willfully try to end his life? I was sane, and a sane person would never attempt suicide. That seemed pretty obvious, didn't it?

Do I have a screw loose? Am I nuts? I wondered.

I lay in my hospital bed that first day feeling as if I had taken the express train to crazy town, certain I would not be a functioning member of society again and seeing no reason to get up.

As I pondered this notion in the psych ward, in between taking proffered pills and speaking with myriad doctors, there was a whole lot of doing nothing. After several hours of lying in bed thinking, my brain hurts, and boredom finally got the better of me. I pulled myself up and walked around the seventh floor to look around.

Having never given thought to who I might see in a psych ward, I initially assumed everyone was like me. Stressed out, overworked, depressed "normal" people who'd taken a wrong turn.

I was wrong.

What I saw surprised me. My fellow residents and I had little in common. I was surrounded by unfortunate folks with severe psychological disorders, not people who'd had a one-time short circuit.

There was the 13-year-old boy who'd gone to town on his arms with a razor blade. We actually spent a decent amount of time playing ping-pong, one of the few activities in the psych ward other than sitting around. Fortunately, at that time I avoided my natural inclination to make a comment like "You have quite a slice."

There was the woman who'd been in the psych unit for the better part of a year because she could not deal with the outside world.

Finally, there was my roommate. I don't recall his name, but in my mind, it was Smokey. Smokey was undergoing electroshock therapy. When Smokey and I first chatted, he seemed fine. He went for a treatment and the next day he was virtually catatonic. I think seeing Smokey was the most jarring interaction I had. Not losing my sense of humor, even in the hospital, I thought to myself, "Well, that was shocking, wasn't it?"

It made no sense to me that I was in the psych ward with these people. Sure, I'd had a major misfire after enduring self-inflicted mental anguish for several years. But when taken in the context of the reason for my anguish, which was hating my job, my new surrounding circumstances were bewildering.

I wanted to be home. I wanted to be with my wife.

None of it made any sense.

How the fuck had I ended up here?

"The more decisions you are forced to make alone, the more you are aware of your freedom to choose."

-Thornton Wilder

I didn't understand it growing up, but I was taught that I didn't have freedom of choice. *Life choices*, specifically, were off the menu.

Looking back, I think that left to my own devices, I would have chosen to be a comic or a musician, or otherwise do something creative. Unfortunately, I never believed it was a real possibility. I was supposed to have a stable job.

I wasn't really even allowed to choose my own feelings unless I chose *happy*. For example, for no particular reason, when I was eleven, I was feeling especially down. Again, I think I've had some level of depression my entire life. At the time, I told my parents I felt depressed. Mom simply replied, "Children don't get depressed."

Me studying at my parent0's house. New City, New York
Circa 1983. What I should have said
when they told me kids don't get depressed.

The Doctor is In

Like many boys, I wanted to be like my father, the doctor. My dad George was a general practitioner, otherwise known back in the day as a "family doctor," the kind who made house calls. Thus, I decided at about age four that I wanted to be a doctor like my old man.

My parents encouraged my desire to be a doctor because they wanted all of their sons to be "professionals," meaning a doctor, a lawyer, or an accountant.

Of course, also like many boys, before I was old enough to shave, I realized Dad's profession might not be for me. I didn't love science and the thought of devoting four years of medical school followed by residency seemed like a bad idea. My parents weren't quite as happy to hear that. I was the youngest of three boys and their real last hope of having another doctor in the family,

Not wanting to be a disappointment, I pushed my own desires aside and convinced myself that being a doctor was what I wanted. I believed I had no choice in the matter. I didn't want to let them down. I remember when I was about nine or ten, I'd think about becoming a cartoonist (I love to draw) or a singer or an actor … something creative. I also remember believing it was too bad those were not options for me.

Think about that for a second. I was a kid, and I believed I didn't have the option to pursue things about which I was passionate. That's a heavy load for a kid to bear.

Fast forward to high school and 11th grade chemistry. I was still holding onto the doctor idea, but I was not at all enthusiastic. By that point, my averageness in science was obvious, but my parents were ignoring that somewhat important fact.

Thankfully, in the middle of the year, my chemistry teacher Mrs. Caruso paved the way for my exit from the medical career path. She assigned the class an unscientific project to break up the monotony of learning the elements. She asked us to write a short narrative story that somehow involved chemistry. It could be anything we wanted. It was a purely creative exercise.

The assignment turned out to be the only A grade I ever received in chemistry. Mrs. Caruso loved the story. She saw my literary promise as her opening and seized the opportunity to take me aside and kindly suggest to me that I would be very good at not being a doctor. My strength was in communication — writing or speaking, but not in science.

Mrs. Caruso was being kind. As an educator, she was trying to guide me.

Mom and Dad did not see it that way. When I told my parents what Mrs. Caruso had said, they were super pissed off about her observation. They even got me riled up.

"Who does she think she is?" they said.

Yeah. "*Fuck her,*" I thought. "*My parents say I can do anything.*"

The seed, however, had been planted.

I survived chemistry my junior year and moved on to physics my senior year, still reluctantly on the pre-med path, having been pulled back by my parents. At the beginning of that year, I also went through the college application process. Through some miracle, I was accepted to the State University of New York at the Stony Brook pre-med honors program (based upon my overall grades — not science alone) and I was leaning toward accepting the offer.

Back in physics, I was academically way out of my depth. I was so far behind in my labs I somehow managed to convince the teacher to let me stand on my head during one class so I would not have to make up the labs. The truth is that he was so fed up with my joke-telling and disruption that he figured I would shut up if all the blood rushed to my head. True story.

At some point that year, I embraced Ms. Caruso's advice and my own instincts, realizing that my parentally designated, super-human ability to do anything in the world excluded being a doctor. I was relieved to decline Stony Brook, deciding instead to take a non-science path at the State University at Albany in New York.

My parents had to accept I was not going to be a doctor. They were disappointed. I was not. I was relieved. I had lost interest in being a doctor many years earlier. I just didn't believe I had a choice in the matter. Thankfully, in this case, the choice was made for me.

But my parents would not be foiled again…

COLLEGE

**"Pay attention, don't let life go by you.
Fall in love with the back of your cereal box."**

-Jerry Seinfeld

Having confidence in yourself and trusting your own judgment is vital. If I could go back and teach young me any one lesson, it would be *Trust your gut.*

When you act or make decisions to please other people, you sell yourself short. You are living in fear of disappointing others. That is a great way to cover up happiness.

My first two years of college were a great example of how I fucked that up.

College

At Albany University in upstate New York, I was an honor student who was also extremely involved in extracurricular activities. For my first two years of college, I enjoyed almost none of it.

53

As a first-semester freshman, I had the unique experience of being the founding president of the Albany chapter of the national fraternity, Alpha Epsilon Pi (AEPi). Our chapter was the first fraternity at the university since the 1960s, and I was running point on the whole damned thing. It was a pretty monumental undertaking for anyone, let alone a freshman.

For me, it was a monumental mistake.

This unique event actually began my senior year of high school, when I was approached to start the chapter by a representative of AEPi's National Office, which identified me through my brother Mo, a brother in the University of Delaware Chapter.

When I was asked to start the chapter, I said yes. At first, I was caught up in the excitement of being courted by the national office while I was still in high school. I was taken out to dinner in New York to meet presidents of other chapters, and was told what a great experience it was. Furthermore, I would be president of the chapter in my freshman year, something very few people could ever claim.

More importantly, I knew it also would make my dad proud. George had been AEPi at New York University back in the day, and I knew it would be a big deal to him. I never really felt like I had a choice.

As September approached, it occurred to me that taking this on as a freshman might be a bit too much for me. I wasn't even sure I wanted to be in a fraternity, let alone president, while still adjusting to college life. My gut was telling me it might not be a good idea for me to take it on as a freshman. Not wanting to disappoint anyone, I ignored it.

As I do with most things, I went in with guns blazing, recruiting everyone from freshmen to seniors, putting together an executive board and dealing with the school, all the while attending classes and trying to make friends.

By the end of my freshman year, we'd recruited a huge, record-setting initiation class of founding fathers — fifty young men ranging in age from freshman to seniors — into the Albany Chapter of AEPi. It was a pretty big deal and I was in charge of it all. You would think I would have had a ton of friends and would be feeling great. It should have been awesome.

Nope.

I never felt comfortable and, if I'm being honest, I don't know how much my fraternity brothers cared for me. I had a big fucking mouth and was not that easy to be around. I was more stressed about it than able to enjoy it and it showed in my words and actions.

There was the time I yelled…

"Hey. This is serious shit!"

…to an auditorium of 200 pretty young women who wanted to be *little sisters* of the fraternity. Everyone was simply enjoying themselves and talking and laughing. I wanted everyone's attention and I nuked it. The assembled brothers appropriately recognized my massive "cock-block" and quickly ushered me to the side.

I felt out of place in the fraternity. I had 50 *brothers* and yet I felt completely alone. Rather than trust my instinct to walk away after my freshman year, I stayed too long because I didn't want to be considered a quitter. Most everyone loved the fraternity, but no one wanted to be in charge, so I stayed on as president my sophomore year. This so-called resilience was a trait that almost killed me as a lawyer.[2]

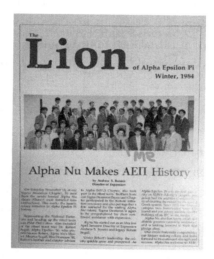

Cover of AEPi's National Magazine, The Lion

---

[2] Lest anyone think I am exaggerating or overstating my involvement in the birth of Albany's Fraternity movement, above is the front page article from AEPi's National Magazine, stating, "Alpha Nu (our chapter name) started out as an idea between {the director of expansion} and legacy Robert Segall. Under Robert's leadership, the {chapter} grew and prospered." I was 18.

By sophomore year I found myself president of a huge fraternity, yet with very few friends in the fraternity.

That first semester of sophomore year was an especially low point for me. Between the fraternity and failing my statistics class, which I'll discuss in another chapter, I had a meltdown midway through my first semester of sophomore year. This again was due to my thoughts running roughshod all over me. *I'm going to fail out of school, I'm a loser* and *I have no friends* were some of the nicer things I was thinking.

My parents wanted me to come home, but somehow I stuck with it and finished out the semester. Pushed to the edge, however, I had to make a change, or another meltdown was imminent.

This theme repeated itself every few years in my life. I committed to something and pushed ahead, even if I didn't like it, thinking I had no other choice. I would then drive myself to the brink of a breakdown.

Up until that that point, my time at Albany consisted of the entire fraternity experiment. It had been quite successful and was a great social outlet for the one-hundred-plus brothers who'd pledged, and many of them remain close friends to this day.

Sadly, for me, it had been a mistake. I remain friends with very few of my fraternity brothers and, in fact, very few people from college. This is an interesting fact given that I have maintained many wonderful friends throughout my life, some from as early as kindergarten. I did not feel happy in college, which caused me to act like an asshole. Quite frankly, not that many people wanted to be my friend.

I've Got the Music In Me

After breaking down during the first semester sophomore year, I finally moved on.

I reached out to the thing that had always been my safety net — singing.

Singing is the one thing that has always uncovered my greatest happiness and provided some of my greatest friendships. It's also something at which I excel. My band won the battle of the bands in high school. I was voted best male singer in my senior class. I met my wife while we were both in the play *Oklahoma*, where I was ironically cast as "Curly." At the time, it was true — I had a major Jewfro.

Oklahoma 1984

Anyway, singing and performing always seemed to bring good things to me.

Back in Albany, my gut told me that finding an outlet to sing was important. This time I listened to myself and pursued my passion.

Midway through my sophomore year, I auditioned for and landed the lead in the university production of the musical *Hair*.

From there, I connected with the guys in the show's backing band and we formed a musical group, 2 Hours Late. While the guys spent far more time getting high than rehearsing (hence the name 2 Hours Late), prematurely ending the band before it really began, it was a great experience and I had the jumpstart I needed.

Midway through my junior year, after the break-up of 2 Hours Late, I heard of a new band looking for a singer. I auditioned for and joined this group, which we named The Difference. That band turned out to be my true college fraternity.

There were six of us — two guitars, a keyboard, bass, drums, and a lead singer. We clicked immediately, and in a short period of time became the go-to party band in a school of over 10,000 people, covering U2, Squeeze, The Cure and any other 80's bands with big hair we could find.

By senior year, we were extremely popular, playing all over Albany, including, ironically enough, huge fraternity parties, having a great time and making some money. I felt fulfilled and it added tremendous happiness to my life. It seemed as if hanging around creative people and performing softened my inherent edge--an edge that caused and would cause me a great deal of trouble later in my life. This edge came out most acutely when I wasn't happy.

My happiest times have always been while performing.
Albany, New York. 1987.

Given my connection to and aptitude for performing, investigating something in the creative arts should have been an obvious choice for a career. It definitely occurred to me. Unfortunately, to the people upon whose counsel I relied, my parents, it was not apparent at all.

Thus, while I entertained the idea of connecting with a band after graduation to take a shot at music, it was never a realistic option. You see, by *entertained*, I mean the way you might look from the top floor down when you are inside a mall and entertaining the idea of jumping. I knew it was never going to happen. I knew it beyond a doubt because I didn't have my parent's sign-off. I never considered it a real choice.

That is all on me. I should have trusted my instincts. I should have listened to myself. I should not have given into fear.

Law and the Aftermath

The Beginning of the End

Rather than investigating other options, upon graduation I enrolled at Brooklyn Law School. My parents insisted that I "get the degree. You don't have to practice." While they were sincere when they said that, we all knew it was kind of bullshit. We were perfectly aware that after three years of law school I would be practicing law somewhere. I certainly didn't believe I had any other choice.

From the start of my first day of law school, everything felt like a burden. Getting out of bed felt like lifting a bag of cement on my back. Every day's burden sent my stress level through the roof. That stress would eventually translate into depression at the prospects for my life.

For me, the experience was mostly suffering, but I assumed at the time that suffering was typical for everyone in law school. I didn't think my interpretation of events was at all unusual. Even though music was my passion, I managed to convince myself I wouldn't have been a successful musician. So why not law? At least law paid well, and that was the important thing, wasn't it?

Not coincidentally, my best memories of law school surround my involvement in the third-year review, otherwise known as "Second Circus." That is where third-year students write comedy humorous skits and songs poking fun at the school and professors. That was one of the only times I was at ease the entire three years.

Often, in times of reflection, I find myself looking back to 1988/89, my first year at Brooklyn law school or, as I affectionately call it, the worst year of my life. Years later, I realized that while I was caught in this self-imposed year of hell, my brain was screaming at me to get out.

I ignored the warning.

Once again, listening to myself was a critical area in which I lacked skill.

The first year of law school dictates what will happen throughout your entire law school career and, believe it or not, potentially the direction of your entire professional life.

The first year is excruciating. The workload is the heaviest and the days don't vary. Your life alternates between studying, sleeping, eating, and going to class. It's like the movie *Groundhog Day* but without the fun, humor, or happy ending. In fact, it was the opposite.

You end up a lawyer.

To make things even worse, the competitiveness amongst first year students is fierce, which creates an intensely stressful environment of its own. I fought through each day with a knot in my stomach fueled by fear, stress and anger that grew with every class I took.

The one oasis for me in the sea of crap was my study group.

During first year, everyone formed study groups, which was generally an assemblage of four to six students who regularly met to discuss and review weekly lessons and prepare for exams. Your study group immediately became your best friends and support system. You laughed, drank, and worked late into the night every week.

Toward the end of the first semester, we had all worked our asses off for almost four months and were tired and stressed. All we wanted was for exams to be over so we could have a much-needed break for a few weeks before starting the whole process over again.

One evening, as we were finishing up a study session, something in me snapped. The stress got the better of me and I blurted out a question that seemed utterly insane but, in hindsight, was the most logical thing I had said all year. It was my brain trying to save me.

"What if it's wrong?" I asked.

"What?" my buddy Dave replied.

"What if it's all wrong? What if everything in our study guides is all wrong? What if…?"

Bam!

As if a boulder fell from the sky and floored me, I remember this thought. I remember asking,

"What if it's all wrong?"

My study group partners looked at me as if I were high. With vacant, blank, lifeless stares they ignored my question. It was if I had asked, "What if our heads explode during the exam?" It was utter nonsense. They simply ignored me and moved on.

I believe the question I was asking was entirely different than what I meant, and had nothing to do with our study guides. It had to do with my choosing law school.

My brain sent me these goddamned encrypted messages instead of just saying *Hey Rob. You know, if you are this unhappy, maaaaybe law is not the right thing for you.*

Again, I didn't listen.

"It's the end of the world as we know it."

-R.E.M.

In May of 1991, after three long years, I finished law school with good grades and unfortunately passed the New York State Bar Exam on the first try. That sealed my fate.

Worst Day of My Life. Law School Graduation. New York City. 1991.

With solid academic credentials and excellent interviewing skills, I secured a job directly out of law school at the mid-sized securities law firm of Spengler, Carlson, Gubar, Brodsky and Frischling. That posed a new dilemma.

From the very first day, I was completely out of my depth. The work was excruciatingly boring. Securities law, explained very loosely, involves S.E.C. regulations. Basically, it's investment-related law. It is dry stuff on a good day, and to me, it was complete fucking drudgery every day. I felt as if a ball and chain had attached itself to my brain.

I did my best to soldier on. After all, the job paid very well and at that time jobs weren't easy to come by. I was one of the lucky ones.

You may be wondering why I applied for a job I didn't want, let alone accepting an offer of full-time employment. The answer boiled down to timing and economics.

The process by which law students acquire their horrible jobs is interesting, if not logical. It begins during your second year.

During second year of law school, a finite number of potential employers agree to conduct on-campus interviews for "associate" positions to be filled for the summer between the second and third year of law school. Those over-paid internships are what often lead to full-time employment upon graduation.

The strategy is to submit the maximum allowable number of resumes, and then cross your fingers and pray that at least one firm wanted to interview you.

If you weren't able to secure a job through the on-campus process, your job prospects still existed, but the options weren't as lucrative, and it made the search far more difficult.

If all the stars align, you secure a high-paying permanent job before even finishing school.

The top students always secured several on-campus interviews, while most everyone else was lucky to be asked to meet with one firm. I was somewhere in the middle. I had solid grades but not top grades, so I wasn't certain I would even get an interview.

To my surprise, I was invited to interview on campus with three firms, two of which invited me back for second interviews in their offices. With more than half of the applicants not even securing one on-campus interview, this was a huge deal for me.

The first firm I visited had the warmth of the American Nazi party, so when I received their rejection letter, I wasn't overly disappointed. The second firm, the aforementioned Spengler Carlson, was much more pleasant. The interview went well, and I eventually was made an offer, which I immediately accepted.

That leads to the economics part. In 1991, my final year of law school, the job market was very tight. Law firms were closing in record numbers due to a combination of overexpansion and a severe downturn in the economy.

I suppressed the fact that I had no interest in that firm's area of specialty because I needed a job. Karin and I were engaged, she had one more year of school to complete, and the compensation the firm offered was very good, so taking that job felt like a no-brainer. I never even tested the waters outside of the on-campus interview process.

One area there was opportunity outside of the law firm sector was at the four surrounding district attorneys' offices. I actually was very interested in the DA because it offered real-time trial experience.

Those jobs, however, didn't pay nearly as well. My fear left me with no confidence in myself and I didn't listen to my gut feelings. Karin, on the other hand, had all the confidence in the world in me and never, not even once, mentioned the money. She would have been fine with the district attorney's office or, quite frankly, anything. She wanted me to be happy.

Taking that job at Spengler Carlson was a pivotal event in my life. It came at a time when my fear-based thinking was at its worst. I believed I would never get an offer that good and that I was "lucky" to be paid well to do something I hated. In hindsight, I know this mindset was extremely limiting, but I only learned that much later.

Take the job. Make the money. I'll be okay. I'll figure it out.

Taking a job solely for the money made the pain and discomfort I felt in law school seem like child's play. This was a brand-new type of suffering.

Living the Dream

In the fall of 1991, it looked as if I was living the American dream. I was a twenty-five-year-old lawyer working in my first job at a well-regarded, prestigious mid-sized law firm in Manhattan. I was married to my beautiful high school sweetheart Karin, who was in her third year of law school and had already secured a job after graduation with a large, extremely prestigious New York City law firm.

We lived in an apartment in Brooklyn Heights overlooking the Manhattan skyline — if you leaned to the left while looking out of the window. Okay, we were just starting out. Objectively it was pretty damn perfect.

Lawyers in Love. Honeymoon in Aruba. 1991.

We were on the ladder to success. Our next step was to save to buy a home in the suburbs. We were young and in love, we had good jobs and the future was at our feet.

Life was good and yet I couldn't see it. I was becoming increasingly miserable and depressed with every day that passed by the prospects for my life. I couldn't see how good most of my life was. No one other than Karin knew the chaos inside me and even she didn't know the full extent of my wretchedness.

I was in a job I despised, surrounded by a group composed mostly of pompous Ivy-League educated lawyers who assumed they were smarter than me (which they were). I could not have felt more miserable. I suffered along, collecting a paycheck and numbly walking through each day waiting for it to end and fantasizing about getting the hell out of there.

My tipping point came one winter day in December of 1991. I'd had a startling and upsetting moment of clarity. I don't know why it hit me at that particular moment, but while in the firm's library, bored out of my mind researching a mundane issue for a partner, a frightening idea struck me like a lightning bolt.

At that moment, I realized, *I don't want to be a partner in a law firm. I'm doing the wrong thing. Why am I here?*

That's when the panic and depression that had been simmering bubbled up and took over. That was the beginning of the end for me.

Once again, I missed an opportunity to listen to myself.

My brain was shouting a call to action. I should have quit, or at least started charting an alternate course. In my state of constant fear, however, that did not appear possible to me. My parents had leveraged themselves to pay for my education, plus I had endured three years of law school and the bar exam. I honestly didn't think quitting was an option.

Choice.

I felt I had none. That is the destination to which my thoughts always arrived.

In early 1992, I received the greatest news ever — the firm announced it was letting go of its entire first-year class of associates because of a merger with another firm. I was relieved because I felt like any change would help. I started interviewing.

Once again, thanks to strong communication skills, my interviews went well, and I quickly found another job at a decent law firm — Lester, Schwab, Katz, and Dwyer. I was better suited for this new firm's insurance litigation practice and a stable of similarly educated law lawyers. I figured this might be a good home for me. I felt positive for the first time in a while.

That warmth and fuzziness wore off in about two months, at which point I became even more unhappy than I had been at Spengler. Here I was at a firm specializing in work I found more interesting, yet I was still miserable. I suppose I shouldn't have been surprised. Neither the law nor I had changed. I was still involved in the petty arguing of civil litigation. I was still surrounded by lawyers. I had never wanted to be a lawyer in the first place. All of this was lost on me because in my mind, this was what I was supposed to be doing. What other options did I have?

I was failing.

I stuck it out for a year and a half and then once again changed firms, this time to Ohrenstein and Brown, making it three law firms in four years.

I continued hoping it was the law firm and not the law itself or something internal that was causing my anxiety. I simply refused to accept the notion that I had chosen wrong, or to entertain the idea that I was not suited to be a lawyer, because that would make me a failure.

Things quickly went from bad to worse. I was caught in a downward mental spiral. I had trouble functioning and thinking clearly. I'd involuntarily start shaking out of nowhere and would sweat for no reason. I had panic attacks several times daily.

The worst part, the part that made me want to die, was that I saw no end to this misery. I did my best to suck it up, but no matter how hard I tried, my efforts were deficient. I was an absolute mess when I got up in the morning. I was now shaking uncontrollably and punctuating everything I said with a heavy sigh.

There was little that Karin could do to stop my mental freefall. She had just put herself through college and law school and was starting her career. Like anyone at that stage in their lives, her focus was supposed to be on her professional journey, not in babysitting me.

Nevertheless, there she was, fielding my frantic calls every day from work, listening to me complain, hearing the heavy sighs around the apartment and feeling the bed shake as I twitched from nerves. All she could do was tell me it would be okay, even though she wasn't at all sure that was true.

Moving On Up

Our intention had always been to move out of the city and have children. I hoped those two things might break this cycle of anxiety I was experiencing.

Our First Home. Dobbs Ferry, New York

Our plan was to have a couple of kids, eventually move into a bigger house, and spend the next forty or so years practicing law. My brain had been trying to tell me to slow down, but I ignored it. The result was that our plans and my life were almost permanently derailed.

In June of 1994, we purchased our first home, a townhouse in Dobbs Ferry, a suburb of Westchester. While I loved being outside the city, it did nothing to abate my feelings regarding being a lawyer. I hated it more each day and grew increasingly more despondent.

In the fall of 1995, we learned that Karin was pregnant. This was right on schedule with our plan. I was as happy as my brain allowed, but not nearly as happy as I should have been.

"I'm going off the rails on a Crazy Train."

-Ozzie Osbourne

Every morning, five days a week, Karin and I took the Metro North commuter train together into Grand Central Terminal in Manhattan. The commute was my daily descent into hell.

It would start out pleasantly enough with Karin and me sitting side by side reading the newspaper and drinking coffee as the train wound its way from Dobbs Ferry down the west side of Westchester County and into the city. The track runs along the shore of the Hudson River and objectively was scenic and peaceful.

I didn't notice any of it.

The closer we got to the tunnel leading to Grand Central Station from Metro North's outdoor tracks, the more severe my anxiety grew. As we approached the tunnel and I saw the outside world about to disappear, my heart quickened, my forehead beaded with sweat and I felt increasingly out of control.

It was like beginning each day on a rollercoaster. The opening of the tunnel was the mouth of a monster waiting to swallow me up into the darkness as the train twisted and turned, ultimately stopping at the end of the line. Unlike an amusement park ride, however, the end of the line was not filled with excitement, relief, and desire to do it again. Instead, it was filled with a desire to shit myself.

My pulse would race as we pulled into the station. As I exited the train and began walking toward my office, my pace would slow considerably, weighted down by dread.

The only thing I hated more than the thirty-minute train ride into work was where I was headed — working as a lawyer in a profession where I felt lost, out of place, and progressively more unhappy every day.

The Beginning of the End

In March of 1995, Karin miscarried. I have very few regrets in life,[3] but I very much regret that I was not there for her when it happened. I was too completely wrapped up in my own shit. If I am being honest, while I was sad for us and particularly Karin, I probably felt relieved, because I didn't feel capable of caring for a baby at that time. I don't remember feeling that way per se, but I cannot imagine I felt the same level of sadness as Karin because I was just fucking numb.

Thinking back, this really sucked for her in a way that would have broken most people. Not only was I a fucking

---

[3] I know what you are thinking. We will address my feelings about my suicide attempt in a later chapter.

mess, but the one good thing for her at that time, a baby, had eluded her while I had pretty much checked out. I still don't know why she didn't tell me to go fuck myself and kick me out. I can't believe how strong she was.

My emotions were out of control and I just wanted it to stop. Like so many people suffering from depression and/or anxiety, the thought of permanently ending my pain started to look like relief.

The thoughts slowly crept into my head as I fantasized about being done with it all. The idea quickly gained traction. I imagined jumping in front of a bus. I actually tried one time at the corner of Vanderbilt and 45th Street, but I couldn't take that last step. I was afraid I would just end up disabled. Pills seemed the least painful way to check out, and I had access to pills. I had been taking medication for a couple of years at this point to control the anxiety and depression.

I guess I thought about it long enough that I convinced myself suicide was rational and made sense. Ultimately, I decided there was no other option.

It Was the End of the World As We Knew It

On April 12, 1995, Karin and I boarded the train into work together as always. Months later, she told me that as we parted ways in Grand Central Station that morning, I seemed more hesitant than usual to separate. She was right. I believed I would never again see her.

I proceeded to my office at 230 Park Avenue, the Helmsley Building, across the street from Grand Central Terminal. I slowly entered the elevator and pressed the button for the 32nd floor. As the elevator ascended, I felt an odd mix of fear and relief — fear of death, but relief that a burden was lifting off me. I thought I was about to end all my pain.

I exited the elevator, walked in through a side door and then into my office. Once inside, I closed my office door, sat down at my desk, and opened the bottles of pills I took for anxiety and depression. After a moment or two of deliberating, I emptied the entire contents of both bottles into my mouth, took a few swigs of water and swallowed. I think it was around thirty or so pills.

The next thing I did was call my mother. That had not originally been my intention. I just did it. My conscious plan was to close my eyes and die at my desk. My subconscious mind, however, which had orchestrated this entire event, had different plans from the start.

Facing the Music

Back on the phone, my mom hung up on me and immediately called for my dad, who frantically called the law firm. Imagine having to call your adult child's place of work to tell them your son was dying in his office. What a horrible task. It was years later before I considered how terrible that must have been for them.

Dad reached one of the partners at the firm, who rushed into my office and hustled me into an elevator. I vaguely remember him loading us into a cab but recall nothing of the ride to NYU Hospital on 1st Avenue. I'd blacked out.

Over time, I understood that my attempted overdose was the proverbial cry for help. I wanted out of law and was too ashamed and embarrassed that I could not make it as a lawyer to simply quit.

**"I've learned that people will forget what you said,
people will forget what you did,
but people will never forget how you made them feel."**

-Carl W. Buehner

When I awoke, I found myself lying on a bed in an emergency room at New York University Medical Center on the lower east side of Manhattan. My stomach had been freshly pumped and my family was standing over my bed looking worried and angry. It felt a little like the scene in the *The Wizard of Oz* where Dorothy wakes up surrounded by Auntie Em and the rest of the family. If Dorothy had been a 29-year-old, depressed, suicidal, balding Jewish lawyer who'd tried to overdose, it would have been identical.

Once I was stable, they moved me up to the 7th floor, behind the locked doors of the psychiatric unit. While I was not officially "committed" to staying, I doubt there was any way they would have let me leave.

ROBERT SEGALL, JD

The Psych Ward

When you are in a psychiatric unit of a hospital, in between therapy sessions and meals, there is a lot of doing nothing. In many ways that was liberating. It was the first time I could remember I had nothing to do. No studying, working, paying bills, jumping in the car, researching, going to meetings, making phone calls...*nothing*.

Sitting alone looking out at the East River and thinking about my life without the daily pressure was a bit surreal. It wasn't just the meds taking effect. It was the nothingness. Space and time didn't really exist. I didn't have to think about work, or really, anything at all.

I spent my time alone in a small lounge, which was just an empty extra room, appointed with a tired-looking, old-cushioned chair and an antiquated exercise bicycle. The one plus was a window with an incredible view of the East River. There I would sit, either in the chair or on the floor on the worn carpet, staring out the window, mindlessly eating the peanut M&M's my family had brought me, and not really thinking much about my next step or what I had to accomplish that day for one of the law firm's partners.

At that moment, I felt a temporary sense of relief. I was relaxed for the first time in a long time. For that that brief moment, I wasn't pushing and felt just a bit freer. One thing I knew for certain — I was saying goodbye to law, something that was of no use to me.

Of course, I also knew that was bullshit. I had a wife I loved whom I hoped would stay with me, and suddenly I had no career.

Being Patient

An incident in the hospital drove this point home. In this moment, my relief came to an abrupt halt and I was reminded I was in a fucking psychiatric ward.

The lowest point in my life came in front of group of young resident doctors midway through my stay at NYU. NYU is a teaching hospital. This means they brought students into the various areas of the hospital to observe patient treatments, make diagnoses, etc. A few days after I was admitted to the hospital, one of teachers, a psychiatrist, asked if I would mind being observed by a class while he asked me questions. He had examined me previously and had concluded I was a situational, short-stay patient. I was the rare patient who could interact with him "normally" and answer questions without melting down, or so he thought.

I was quite bored at this point, so I said yes (as usual), which, in hindsight wasn't such a great idea.

That day, I sat at the front of a tiered lecture-style classroom, much like the lecture centers at colleges — semi-circular with rows of elevated seats going back. I was at the bottom with the professor, answering his questions.

The doctor interviewed me for several minutes, asking questions about what had led to my fateful decision and why I'd taken that path. A few minutes into the interview, I glanced up in the back of the room to see some cocky-looking young male doctor whispering into the ear of a giggling female doctor. I have no idea what they were discussing. It probably wasn't me. But I did know how cold it was.

I lost my temper. I lost it right there in front of thirty or forty young doctors all around my age. In tears, I stopped what I was saying, looked up at them and yelled, *"Do you think this is funny? This could easily be you! This is my fucking life and you are up there laughing and telling secrets?! How dare you."*

The doctors looked sufficiently chastened. At that moment, I realized how far I had fallen. I was a subject of a medical school psychology class being looked upon with pity—or worse. I felt two inches tall.

That moment still has an enormous impact on me all these years later. The memory remains vivid, both in its insensitivity and as a reminder of how my low thoughts drove me to a psych classroom as a subject in a mental hospital.

Just like the moment when I stood in that law library during my first law job at Spengler Carlson and realized I had devoted myself to a career I didn't want, sitting in that classroom in the hospital, I realized how badly I had fucked up.

Yet another tipping point. The overdose had solved nothing. It was the culmination of years of severe anxiety, self-doubt, raging fear, and extreme bouts of depression. It had temporarily relieved some of my pain. That was it.

After a seven-day stay I was considered stable. There was nothing more I would get out of spending more time in the ward. I had cured nothing, but I was out of the hospital.

And (almost) out of law.

"You shouldn't be fearful of starting over."

-Jeffrey Katzenberg

When I think back to this time in my life, I don't have much recollection of what occurred after returning home to Dobbs Ferry and starting up work again. I know it was a short period of time. Karin never judged me, so I don't remember any big blow-out or argument. I have no memory of her getting angry, nor of her pushing me away.

One of the other things I regret was not considering the pain my actions caused Karin. I thrust her into this situation, and I don't think anyone really asked how she was feeling. Everyone focused on me, and she had to deal with her feeling of abandonment on her own.

Rather than lashing out at me as most people would have done, it was the opposite. She made sure I knew she still had faith in me, loved me, and wanted to start a family, something we did one year later.

Her empathy is still so remarkable to me that I feel it bears restating. I wouldn't have made it through this difficult period in my life without her lifting me up.

Back to Law

As for reengaging, as odd as it may seem, I wasn't immediately unemployed after being discharged from the hospital. Sitting at home waiting to find the "right" opportunity was the last thing I wanted to do. I didn't want to make a shitty situation worse by looking for a pity party. I wasn't the type of person to curl up in a ball and do nothing. On the other hand, I was the kind of person to take a bunch of pills, so perhaps the curled-in-a-ball thing may have been better.

Maybe a week after being discharged from the hospital, I returned to Ohrenstein and Brown. That may sound odd given that I'd been carried out on April 12th, but they didn't say no when I asked to return, if only to clean things up. I felt I had to ask. We were in a new house and our plans didn't contemplate only one person working. Even though Karin was by far the bigger wage earner and she certainly didn't ask me to rush back to work, I still needed to make money. Also, I knew this time the law job was temporary.

To their credit, the people at Ohrenstein were extremely gracious about letting me come back. They would have let me stay longer despite everyone's obvious and understandable discomfort with the situation. I didn't help the situation when I went to kitchen for a cup of coffee, couldn't find the milk and muttered, "If there's no milk, I don't know what I'll do."

I was able to use my time there to tie up loose ends and give some thought as to what I would do next. Looking back, it took some pretty big balls for me to go back there even for a little while.

Let's Go to the Videotape

Early on, I knew I needed a different entry point back into the working world. I couldn't think of any particular way to make money and had no real end game, I only know that law was no longer an option.

Having no other obvious job or career choices, I made a smart decision and chose love. I called my cousin Jim Lyman, an entrepreneur business owner, and asked him to help me.

Jim is one of those cousins who is more like a brother. I viewed him as the example of how I wanted to live my life going forward. When faced with extremely difficult circumstances, Jim had turned them to his advantage because he'd trusted his gut. It was no surprise that Jim became a big success in every aspect of his life.

Jim lost his father at age four to a heart attack and his mother when he was age 20. Not knowing where to go, he moved in with my parents for a bit while he tried to figure out what he was going to do. He and I grew close during that time. Of course, my parents tried to persuade Jim to complete college and possibly law school, like his dad. Fortunately, Jim was strong enough to ignore that shitty advice and follow his instincts, which served him well throughout his life.

After I was out of the hospital, I called Jim to see if he might have something for me jobwise. He didn't hesitate in saying yes despite not really having a position available for me. He created one and figured it out from there so he could help me.

At that time, Jim owned a wholesale video distribution business, *J & I Video*, in White Plains, a city about thirty minutes north of Manhattan. It was an easy drive (no train!) from my home and was staffed by Jim, his sister (my cousin) Melissa and a few others who were mostly hardworking and fun to be around.

It may make you chuckle in the world of streaming to think about a video business, but remember that it was 1995 and videotapes were still the primary means of watching most everything. There was no streaming. This included pornography. Unlimited pornography and attendance at an adult video convention turned out to be job perks.

J & I, which ultimately became the successful *View Entertainment*, was a great spot for me to reengage. My days were filled with laughter and purpose in its decidedly noncorporate atmosphere. By non-corporate, I mean wearing jeans or shorts, cursing, and participating in the occasional wrestling match or video case fight.

I loved it at *J & I*. It gave me time to detoxify from the law experience and understand there was a big world out there. I learned that not everyone was, nor needed to be, a professional (meaning doctor, lawyer, or accountant) to be successful. It opened my mind to new possibilities.

I made myself as useful as possible, doing whatever work needed to be done, be it minor legal work, sweeping floors, working in a warehouse, or learning how to sell.

Theoretically, I was successful. I created a library division, selling previously owned videos to lending libraries. (No porn.)

The idea was good in theory. A part of J & I's business was purchasing entire inventories of defunct retail video stores and reselling them. Jim bought videos for pennies on the dollar and then resold them. He had the idea that libraries would be a great avenue in which to redistribute the videos. At that time, libraries actually had large video lending libraries. At Jim's suggestion, I started a division that sold videos to library branches all over the northeast, including accounts such as the Philadelphia Public Library System. This all sounds impressive in theory, but in dollars, not so much. I didn't really understand the part about profit, which made the Library Division less useful to J & I.

On the upside, I learned that I enjoyed the sales process and was good at it.

I might have stayed at J & I forever were it not for the money. Because I had no real experience that could be particularly useful to Jim at that time, and he'd already done what he could for me by creating a job he didn't actually need, it was just not enough.

I worked at J & I for two years, from 1995-1997, until Karin, who had been more than patient with me, gently but firmly explained that I might need to find something with a bit more of an upside, especially now that we had our daughter, Pamela. Karin was right, and frankly, I was ready.

At this point, remember that I'd quickly jumped back into work after being in the hospital. I didn't give myself any real time to process what had happened and why I'd done it. I just wanted to be involved in something other than my problems.

As a result, the demons that had directed me to overdose still had not been defeated.

**"Things turn out best for the people
who make the best of the way things turn out."**

-John Wooden

Cowan Financial Group

In the spring of 1997, it was time for me to look at my next step. *J & I Video* had given me as much as possible, but it was never meant to be my final spot.

As I considered my next move, and with no real direction, another cousin, Corey Rabin, proactively reached out to help me.

Corey was another person I greatly admired. He also had overcome his own challenges to become a very successful successful as an attorney and real estate investor. More than professional success, the thing I admired most about Corey was his desire to help others. Corey approached life as if he had two full-time jobs: the first was how he made money, and the second was how he could help people. Corey was always looking for ways he could help people through acts of kindness and love.

I have applied Corey's example in my life. That's the type of person I've always tried to be. I believe that when you live thinking about how you can give back, which many people refer to as living in abundance, good things come to you. I know that whatever I've achieved in my life was a direct result of living this way. People have always been there for me in my times of need because I had been there for them without expectation of return.

I learned that helping others significantly enhances happiness.

I think you'll be good at this

Corey knew I was looking around for something and asked me to lunch to discuss an idea. He had an advisor at an insurance and investment firm, Cowan Financial Group, located at 530 5th Avenue in the heart of midtown Manhattan. Corey felt that Cowan, or a place similar to that, might be a good fit for me. Knowing my personality, Corey thought I would do well in sales.

He'd worked with one of the agents at Cowan, Irv Rosenberg, who invited me in for a chat. Irv was a pretty typical old-school insurance guy. By the time we met, he was already in his seventies and looked even older, with a prodigious belly, suspenders to hold up his pants, and a jovial demeanor. What struck me was how much he fucking loved the insurance business. His enthusiasm for the product and the business piqued my interest as we sat in his cluttered office talking over coffee.

While Irv alone didn't sell me on Cowan (he was too fucking old), he did introduce me to several young people with whom I "interviewed."[4] The guys I met were all, for the most part, around my age, and everyone appeared to be

---

[4] Meaning I had a pulse.

motivated and very successful, sitting in big offices wearing custom-made suits.

As I chatted with a few of these young all-stars and voiced my unease at knowing little about financial products, I was assured that it wasn't too difficult to catch on, and that the training was the best in the industry. I could make nice money and be my own boss.

But there's a Catch

I would later learn that the lads I'd met on my interview, while indeed successful, were the extreme minority of people who managed to survive the first few grueling years in the business. I was unaware of the sea of hundreds of other people who'd tried and failed at Cowan and elsewhere. I'd only been exposed to the winners.

It turned out that Cowan Financial Group was a microcosm of the financial services industry as a whole, which followed the recruitment model of throwing as much shit against the wall as possible and seeing what would stick. I'd venture that when I started in 1997, maybe 10-15 percent of new salespeople made it past the first year, if that.

When the call came (there was virtually no email yet) with an employment offer from my new sales manager, I was blissfully unaware of the shitstorm I was about to endure. I was elated to be an associate as Cowan. I knew they must have been impressed with my legal background to choose me over the other candidates.

It was either that or because I owned a suit.

After interviewing at a few other similar firms for a point of comparison, I chose Cowan.

Coach Cowan

The firm was run by Howard Cowan. Howard had a sign on his desk that said Coach Cowan, which is ironic if you know him. My opinion is that his coaching style was more Donald Trump from his "The Apprentice" days than Phil Jackson.

Howard built this behemoth firm known throughout the industry for its tremendous success, as well as Howard's take-no-prisoners approach to his sales force. It was essentially an atmosphere of you produced or you didn't matter. Frankly, this was how all insurance firms worked. Howard was just much better at it than everyone else. Cowan Financial was the standard by which insurance firms throughout the country judged themselves.

Howard bred success through a mixture of hard work, purposeful displays of personal wealth meant to motivate his army, and intimidation. As one less-than-successful colleague once explained it, *Cowan Financial Group* was a great place in which to be a success but a crappy place if you wanted to make living. Only the strong survived, and many people became successful under his leadership. As a soldier in his army, I can attest that many of us preferred to walk the other way when we saw him in the hallway if we were having a bad sales month.

In 2000, I had not been in the business long, but the stars aligned, and I had a truly spectacular production year. I was held up as the example of what someone new in the business could accomplish...until 2001.

That was when the tech bubble burst on Wall Street and the bottom fell out of my business. I was crushed and wanted to quit.

Not only was I no longer an example of what could be accomplished, I was ridiculed by colleagues because during my successful year I became an insufferable dick (which illustrates another lesson — be careful how you treat people on the way up. They are the same people you will pass on the way back down).

That October, Howard saw me in the hallway and said loudly for all to hear, "Hey, Segall. What are you going to do when I move you out of that office and back into a cubicle?"[5]

Anyway, all that happened later. I left the office after my interviews feeling that it sounded pretty glamorous and hoping to receive an offer of employment.

The prospect of choosing my own hours and making good money simply by talking to people appealed to me. Additionally, I had no other viable options and I didn't want to sell copiers.

First Day of School

I started in June of 1997 in a class made up of twenty young men, mostly five-to-ten years younger than my thirty-one years.

---

[5] While not germane to the main point of this chapter, my response bears repeating. After Howard's intimidation attempt, I gently guided him onto an empty office, closed the door and said, "Howard, I have been here three years. I quit law because of the stress. If you think I am going to lose sleep over an office, you have learned nothing about me. Let me know when you want me to move." He let me stay and I never really had another bad year after that. I may not have been his top producer, but I always did well.

We were brought into a fancy conference room adorned in dark wood, with leather seats and a grand conference table running the entire length of the room. At that point, after introducing ourselves and feeling nervous but excited with anticipation, we were greeted by…a loud, super-obnoxious, douchebag of a sales manager in a three-piece suit with slicked-back hair who looked like a leg breaker in a Martin Scorsese movie. Then he proceeded to ridicule us as if we were army privates in basic training or pledges in a fraternity.

After the hazing was done and we'd gone through some initial training, we were ushered into *the bullpen*, the place we would call home for the foreseeable future - a windowless room that smelled like ass, filled with cubicles where we were told to *smile and dial.*

It turned out that *financial advising* actually meant sitting in this fart-filled room, throwing shit at each other while making calls from company directories stolen from the lobbies of buildings where we wanted to peddle our wares.

The idea was that on a twenty-second telephone call, you had to persuade a stranger to meet with you by convincing him either that you had met before or that you worked with other people at his firm (neither of which was ever true). The call ostensibly was to see if: "we could chat in person about the planning work we do the next time I am in your office."

Nobody told me about that part. Really fucking glamorous.

That essentially was the crux of the job. We were cold-calling to talk about life insurance and investments. Furthermore, the truth was that the "next time I would be in the office," would be the first time — if the guy on the other end of the line actually agreed to meet me. If he did, I had to find an available senior person to come with me because I didn't know my ass from a hole in the ground in the insurance world. The senior person would then do all the talking. If the prospect bought, we split the commission. This was called *joint work*.

This was my life for a solid year. It sucked. I was making little money and felt lousy about my prospects. I remember one time, after another crappy appointment, staring out of the window in the reception area of a law firm where the person I'd travelled across the city to meet was too busy to see me, with tears in my eyes, wondering what I was going to do. I had a kid at home and literally no idea if this job would work out.

I had been a practicing attorney at a good firm with an office on Park Avenue. I was now sitting with a bunch of mostly unmotivated guys in room that smelled like my butt, calling strangers.

Success?

Sometimes being the type of person who does not give up until I have a breakdown is helpful. It pushed me through the very toughest beginning parts of the business and into the parts that were actually great, where you get to help people and make money.

By the grace of God (and getting in at 6:30am and not leaving before 8:00pm) in my first year, I managed to make enough cold calls and joint work to get enough appointments to make enough sales and get out of my cubicle into a shared office. The people I met were satisfied enough to provide me referrals to colleagues and friends so my stint with cold calling ended pretty quickly. From there

I was off to the races — at least professionally, and later on financially.

More Problems

As to my mental state, remember that after the hospital I jumped right back into the work force with *J & I*, which was low stress (and low pay) into financial services, which is production-based and completely high stress. Meanwhile, other than seeing a therapist for a short while, I had not addressed my anxiety issues. I was still a prisoner of my thoughts.

So, while I began experiencing more professional success than I expected, my anxiety level went haywire. Many mornings I would arrive in the office completely obsessed with *succeeding*, all the while comparing myself to others, which is exactly what they wanted. Our production numbers were publicized on a wall for everyone to see by the ring-master, Howard Cowan, in the hopes that it would drive us insane.

Many early mornings I would have to go into a conference room, lock the door, shut off the lights, and lie on the floor until I could calm myself down. Thankfully, I never got caught.

While the conference room thing passed after the second year, from years two-to-15 it took me a good two to three hours each evening to calm myself down from my self-induced stress.

I tried everything from medication, to therapy, to coaching, but nothing really took hold on its own. My happiness was pretty covered up at this point.

I was once again a complete slave to my thoughts, which led to ever-increasing trouble.

Oops! I did it again!

While I was freaking out on the inside, on the outside, my mouth was up to its old tricks. This caused me repeated problems

For example, maybe a month into my stay, while walking in the office, I encountered Rick, a senior advisor, in the hallway. In addition to being extremely successful and a good guy, another fun fact about Rick was he had recently married his wife Patti, who happened to be a beautiful, successful model. Rick and I had not been formally introduced, but I knew about Patti. He had seen me around, so he stopped and said, "Hi, I'm Rick."

To which I immediately replied, "I know. Tell your wife I left my socks in your apartment."

The list of things I said and did similar to this wisecrack was endless.

I would page fictitious people on the company intercom system, including Hue Jorgan and Phil McCrevis. And of course, I often took over internal meetings at the office with highly inappropriate jokes.

Ultimately my mouth got in the way at work. I was definitely left out of some important moves because of my vocal unpredictability.

Fortunately, I was good at my job, so they kept me around. It was way too much work to find another person who could succeed selling insurance. In Howard's defense, as much as I probably annoyed him, he let me do my thing. As long as you produced, he pretty much left you alone. His approach was meant just as much to help us hit our own personal financial goals as it was for his firm to finish "first" (something always very important to Howard). He took true pleasure when one of his people did well.

As I write this, I thought about why I had not run into similar problems with my mouth when I'd been a lawyer. I think the only reason I avoided the same repercussions at my other places of employment was that I had not been anywhere long enough to properly piss off anyone and was too stressed to be funny.

While my story begins with my suicide attempt, most of my struggle to be happy took place during my twenty-three years selling insurance.

Postscript

I believe sometime around 2005, Howard finally retired.

Cowan Financial Group was taken over by a few of the most successful advisors at the firm, who rebranded it and staffed it with teams of professionals in every discipline. The firm, rebranded Lenox Advisors, is leading national financial advisory firm.

Licensed to Kill

As I close the section of this book on my personal history, I want to make a final, somewhat unrelated point.

When I began in the business, I used to joke that I was licensed to do the two things people hate the most — practice law and sell insurance. While this may be a joke, I know what my colleagues and I do is one of the most important jobs in the world.

Think what you want about lawyers, but I consider professionals selling insurance and other financial products to be unsung heroes.

They're heroes because so many people don't understand the importance of what they do, yet they fight through the misinformation espoused by hucksters and others to make sure families and businesses are protected. They shine a light on these errors, and then correct the mistakes made based on misinformation, fear, and apathy. Mistakes that, if not corrected, cause tremendous pain and hardship for families.

That is all I will say on the subject, but I wanted to make sure I addressed it. If you don't agree, all I can say is *good luck*.

HAPPINESS

I have divided the second half of this book into two sections, both of which provide lessons I've learned about happiness:

1) **The Problems Impacting Happiness:** In order to avoid problems, you need to know what potential problems exist and those actions which cause them, as well as the traps that suck us into covering up our happiness.

2) **The Solutions Uncovering Happiness:** These are the strategies I have used to enjoy my greatest happiness most thoroughly.

There is no particular order to the lessons in each section. At different times, they have all been valuable to me in their own ways. Their importance in my life changes almost daily as there are different things I need to remember when I face different challenges.

While the lessons don't directly relate to each other, combined they've created a roadmap to a better me. Most of them I didn't conceive. I interpreted them and maybe added a thing or two, but the ideas have been around a lot longer than you or me.

I hope you find them helpful.

THE PROBLEMS

"Happiness is determined more by one's state of mind than by external events."

— Dalai Lama XIV, The Art of Happiness

Beginning when I was young, I struggled with stress and anxiety. Later, as I entered my late teens/early adulthood, I was visited two or three times by intense bouts of depression stemming from my anxiety.

For much of my life, my brain's main work product, my thoughts, completely dominated my life. The problem was that while the product was defective, I kept consuming it.

I was in 6th grade. I had been out for about one week with the flu. When I returned there was a significant amount of classwork and homework to make up. Then again, I was 11 and a good student, so how bad could it be? The day I came back I had a full-blown, multi-day panic attack where I could not function. It took me several days to come back to Earth.

The event was significant enough that I marked everything in my life for years after as having occurred before or after that incident.

When a company produces a defective product, there is a recall. With human machines, there is no thought recall. Unless we can fix it ourselves, we must use the defective product, which significantly impacts how we operate. When left unchecked, we can break down.

During the first semester of my sophomore year of college, I was failing statistics, a required course for my major. The reality was that over half the class was failing because the teacher was a disaster. All I had to do was drop the class or change to "pass/fail" so a failing grade wouldn't impact my GPA. It happens all the time. Instead, I had a massive breakdown. I had never really failed before and couldn't process it. After recovering, which took quite some time, I changed the course to "pass/fail," failed, retook the class, and graduated with honors. **I could have done that without the breakdown, but didn't see my way through.**

I Think, Therefore I Am

I have always believed my thoughts. From the time I was young, I believed virtually every thought I had was true, many of which were negative, worst-case scenarios. This led me down the path to the overdose. For years afterward, it caused me significant anxiety and a few more breakdowns.

Thoughts can lead to depression.[6] Faulty thinking may be fatal. My experience with depression was that it was based upon irrational thoughts that felt real. I *knew* I had no options so the despair was overwhelming. Getting out of bed was like trying to walk through quicksand with a bag of cement on my back. I had no hope.

Adding to the problem were people continually telling me to *snap out of it* or *get over it*. Mental issues cannot be seen, felt, or heard, so people think it must not be a real affliction. This, in turn, made me feel even worse, because I was certain there was something *wrong with me*. I felt worthless. It eventually just wore me out. Depression coupled with stress almost killed me.

Born this Way

Thoughts complicate the happiness question. Were it not for the inconvenience of thought, happiness would be easy.

I used to wonder, "Are we born happy?" As I dug in and examined my life, I understood I was asking the wrong question.

My unscientific hypothesis is this: We are born with our minds clean. In other words, nothing covers up our happiness. Life makes it impossible to maintain this. As we grow into our teenage years, with greater responsibilities and decisions to be made every day, thoughts distract from our core happiness. Without the

---

[6] Again, I am not referring to every instance of depression, many of which must be medically treated and are beyond the scope of this book.

proper tools and guidance to deal with our thoughts, we cannot properly deal with life. That's when problems occur.

Therefore, I've concluded that the question *Are we born happy?* is imprecise. We are all born with some degree of happiness. The better question is:

How happy are we when we are born?

I believe we are born with our own personal levels of happiness fully intact. Then life covers it up and our thoughts become defective.

Lesson: In your search for happiness, begin with your own mind, not some outside influence. Something is covering up your happiness.

"I cannot change what will happen.
I can only change how I act in the face of it."

-Luthiel

I think of the brain like a coffeemaker. We are born with a pristine filter in our brains. There is nothing in it but mommy's boobs for food, pooping, and sleep. Eating, sleeping, and pooping. That is a truly blissful existence.

Then other people start shitting in our filter.

During our development, our filter clogs with the concerns, worries, anxieties and neuroses of the people with whom we interact. This alters the way we process our own original and unique thoughts.

As we integrate these foreign thoughts together with our own, new beliefs take hold. These hybrid thoughts dictate our behaviors, ideas, attitudes, and emotions, while our minds and personalities are still developing.

Our mental filters are first filled by the initial and most dominant figures in our lives — our parents. There are additional contributing people and elements including siblings, friends, teachers, coaches, significant events, and the environment.

Irrespective of who or what dirtied your mental filter, if you are looking for happiness like me, the challenge is separating your original thoughts from what belongs to others. This is not easy. We've carried them around for so long it seems impossible to tell the difference.

Thanks, Dad

My dad took a big dump in my mental filter. I inherited stress from George. If things were not precisely the way he wanted them, he could not relax. There were times that the littlest detail about the most mundane thing could ruin his mood if it was "important" to him. He looked as if he had to drop a deuce all the time. That sort of behavior dominated my personality for years.

Conversely, when things went the way he wanted, he would relax. You could almost see his blood pressure lowering. Growing up, I assumed this all-encompassing obsessiveness was how we were supposed to conduct ourselves, because that was what was caught in my mental filter.

Later in my life, my first business/life coach explained that this phenomenon had a name. He referred to it as *attachment*.

For me, even after I was out of law for a couple of years and thriving in the financial planning career I had chosen for myself and enjoyed, I was destined for another collapse or two because I was always attached to attaining the next thing, thinking that would make me happy. Which never worked.

I didn't know I had this problem with attachment. When I finally understood the concept, unlearning it was a pain in the ass.

"Attachment is the source of all suffering."

-Buddha

Attachment is an integral part of our respective personalities. Incredibily, while it is a significant source of distress, it's very seldomly considered. I certainly never considered it.

The concept of attachment itself actually isn't difficult to understand. When we decide we "need" something, that we must have it, we have become attached. It could be grades, a relationship, a new car, a better job, sex. Anything.

People feel that attachment provides motivation. In sales, the prevailing school of thought is that if you don't feel you *need it*, you have lost your edge. When athletes train their asses off to win a championship or students attach to grades to try to earn admission to a particular college, they are convinced they must have it.

They are wrong.

It may feel like a need, but it is only a want. Their lives will continue with or without meeting their goal. I attached to success as a lawyer and it nearly killed me.

Literally.

I understand that attachment works for some people. I imagine Michael Jordan, Mia Hamm, Beyonce, or Steve Jobs would have achieved success without attachment.

Aside from their incredible talent, however, I also believe the aforementioned superstars had something many of us do not — the ability to pick themselves up when they failed and only look forward and to truly look at failure as a teaching moment. They actually needed attachment in their lives to fulfill their destinies.

For the rest of us mortals, when we confuse *wanting* something with *needing* something, we run into problems. When we cannot disconnect from a want, that's when attachment goes wrong. When you need a thing and it doesn't happen, what option have you left yourself?

Disconnecting from attachment to outcome was an epic battle for me. It meant accepting myself and all my circumstances without judgment. I couldn't earn, work, love, exercise, play, eat or diet my way to lasting happiness. It meant rewiring my brain.

Twenty-plus years after the concept of non-attachment was first introduced to me, I can finally apply the concept fairly effectively. It took me that long to internalize it.

The Potluck Crew

Karin and I have this wonderful group of friends we all referred to as the "Potluck" friends. Allow me to explain.

Growing up in Rockland County, I was friends with Kenny, Adam, Eric, and Jeff. Kenny and Adam were literally two of the first friends I made in kindergarten — Erik and Jeff, beginning pretty much in high school.

Through some miracle, not only have we all remained friends our entire lives, but our wives — Karin, Cindy, Rhonda, Melinda and Elka - have all become friends. We've travelled together, skied together, and celebrated life events together for the past 25 years or so.

The reason for the name "Potluck" was that it all started out around twenty-five years ago when we decided to have a potluck dinner (where everyone brings a dish) at someone's house. As we had young children and going out was both difficult and expensive, we would switch houses every few months and pick a theme (a holiday or country which would dictate the food). This went on for a long time, until the kids reached college age and we switched to doing it less frequently and more often just the parents eating out together. It has continued to this day.

I cannot think of a bigger blessing than having that. That said, for many years I didn't appropriately enjoy it because I was attached to other things.

Our House, in the Middle of Our Street

The worst (or best) example of my attachment was house envy. I grew up upper middle class in a big home in the suburbs. For me, that was the pinnacle. I was completely attached to the idea that I "needed" a house as big as or bigger than the one in which I grew up. It was a bit of an obsession for me.

Our home in the early years of the Potlucks was quite nice. We had great neighbors and a wonderful backyard and the house was certainly big and nice enough. Wanting a third child, however, it would have been tight. Furthermore, none of that mattered. I was attached to the idea of a particular home. I later came to understand that much of that came from wanting to please my dad.

Anyway, one particular Potluck evening we met at Ken and Rhonda's. They had just built a beautiful new house in Westchester. Their home was the exact type of home I dreamed of owning — a grand center hall colonial. While I was definitely happy for them (Ken and Rhonda are two of the most unassuming people I know) I was angry at myself for being a "loser" for not owning a similar house.

I was so completely obsessed with their big house that it was all I could talk about on the ride home and for afterwards. It was enough that Karin and I both remember it vividly to this day.

I was so fucking attached to a particular idea that I didn't truly enjoy that beautiful Potluck moment with my friends and, truth be told, I was probably not as happy for Ken and Rhonda as I should have been.

I have never told my friends about the envy that detracted from the early years of events for me. I'm embarrassed by it and disappointed that my early Potluck memories were colored by that.

Buzzing

That example was the theme for much of my life and professional career. No matter how well I did, my happiness was constantly covered up. I was always chasing a number or a thing or an event. If I ended up getting what I wanted, it never ever made me happy, and I never gave myself credit. I simply moved on to the next thing I did not have.

It was not a matter of being materialistic. We have always lived within our means and have never made a purchase or done something to keep up with others.

It was attachment to the idea of my self-worth.

When my coach taught me the concept of attachment many years ago, it was a revelation to me. I had never heard of the concept. Internalizing it, however, was going to come much later, so attachment continued to rule my life for a long time thereafter. If I was not working, I was thinking about work or production or goals and I was constantly complaining about them.

After twenty years of enduring this bullshit, one weekend we were doing something with the kids, and Karin said these magical words that have stayed with me:

> *"To me, it seems like work is this constant 'low buzzing' in the background of your brain. It's always there, always happening and always distracting your attention."*

I remember asking whether she thought about work all of the time, as I assumed everyone did. When she told me she did not, I was surprised. Somewhere in my brain, I believed that this obsessive thinking was necessary to have success in life.

Her statement had a big impact on me. I thought about it a lot. Constantly. As I considered the low buzz, I realized I had never fully enjoyed anything. My mind was always somewhere else. Then I considered Karin, who, by comparison, managed to have professional success and be present in whatever she was doing. That was why she didn't have the low buzz in her brain. She was living life the way it was intended.

We live in a goal-oriented, materialistic world. We are bombarded with status images of all forms of media. Our bosses put pressure on us to produce, our parents put pressure on us to achieve, we want to be in a particular friend group or want to purchase a particular thing or go on a trip.

Our world, and I suppose human nature, is designed to feed into want, to need. Understanding this is step one toward non-attachment. We are fighting a bit of an uphill battle there. The buzzing conversation started me thinking the proper way, as did this quote my current coach, Steve Harbaugh, taught me, which is the lesson of this chapter:

Lesson: Comparison is the thief of joy.

That sums up attachment. Comparing where we are with where we want to be or where someone else is. The quote has been attributed to Teddy Roosevelt as well as the Bible. It doesn't matter to me. The message is clear.

**"There is nothing good or bad
but thinking makes it so."**

-William Shakespeare

Everybody thinks. It's what we do with our thoughts that dictates happiness.

After leaving the hospital, I believed it had been my situation — being a lawyer — that had caused my breakdown. That turned out to be bullshit. My breakdown was the result of how I'd handled my situation. In other words, how I thought about it.

The obstacles to my happiness had originated from my brain. My brain, and thus my thoughts, were programmed to please others, which led me to law. My thoughts told me I couldn't be a quitter, so I kept practicing law despite hating the career. My thoughts told me I was a failure after the third law firm, which led me to overdose.

My thoughts ran the show, yet I didn't interpret thinking as the problem. I blew every situation out of proportion, always imaging the worst-case scenario and the resulting horrible consequences. I never ever imagined the best possible results.

135

I construed every thought as reality and didn't consider that maybe my point of view was skewed. Neutral events became catastrophes before the events even occurred. I was going through life *always waiting for the other shoe to drop*, a phrase I uttered many times.

A psychologist friend once explained that a term exists in psychology for this type of thought. It is called *magical thinking*. I simply think of it as torture.

I understand that I did myself no favors by going into law. Had I chosen another path, such as something creative, and that didn't work out, maybe I would have handled things differently. It would have been my choice and I would have accepted it.

Or perhaps I would have had another fucking breakdown.

The trigger to my downward spiral happened to be law practice, but it could have been anything. The question I needed to be asking was, "Why was my reaction so severe?"

Why did it affect me so much more acutely? How did I end up so stressed out, worried, and ultimately depressed that I tried to overdose? I knew that if law had not been the trigger, it would have been something else.

In fact, after I left law and entered into the world of financial advising, the same thought patterns quickly emerged and have tortured me for years.

I needed to know why. That has been my twenty-five-year journey.

Lesson: Thought is the root of unhappiness

We don't control our thoughts, yet we think we do. For most of my life, I believed I was in charge of the thoughts torturing me. I believed I "created" them, so they must be true.

Thoughts are free-flowing, and constantly changing, and have no rules. If you are a person like me who was programmed to worry rather than to hope, then the unpredictability of thought may be your nemesis.

By 1995, I spent all my time listening to and obsessing over my thoughts. My mind became completely cluttered, covering up what turned out to be a deep pool of happiness. I focused on what I *should* be doing rather than what *might make me happy*.

I gave my negative thoughts all my energy, and ultimately, they hijacked my life.

Over time, as I came to realize my thoughts were filled with other people's expectations, I was overwhelmed. I needed a way to segregate out the bad stuff (other people's neuroses I'd inherited) and the real stuff (who I really was.)

The reality was that I needed to fix *me*, not just my circumstances. Once I fixed my mind and the way I thought, my circumstances took care of themselves. Fixing my mind meant understanding where my thoughts originated.

**"There are three masks: the one we think we are,
the one we really are, and the one we have in common."**

-Jacques Long

I used to think people fell into three categories: (1) happy people (2) unhappy people (3) people who want to be happy.

Baby me. Even then I don't quite look happy.
Bronx, New York. 1966

Some people are naturally happy. We all know people who look at the bright side, see mistakes as opportunities to learn and generally have a positive outlook on life. When we think about them, we say things such as, "They are good to be around," or "I enjoy their company."

Others view opportunities as potential failures and generally complain about everything. You see them and think, "Do they ever stop complaining?" or "Are they ever happy?" No matter what happens in their lives, they will be angry, cynical, and pissed off.

Then there is that third group, the anxiety-filled group in the middle who wants to enjoy life more but cannot get past the worry and stress. Most moments in their lives are not as good as they can be, and it wears them out. We see them and think *go away*. I was in that group.

Who are you? Who, who, who, who?

As I wrote the book and thought about this concept, I realized it was incorrect. There are only two groups: (1) happy people and (2) people who want to be happier. There is no unhappy.

My mistake was assuming all the nasty, negative people I've met were unhappy. They aren't. They're just more comfortable in that negative space. Someone we may consider an unhappy, cynical, complaining jerk may actually feel good all the time. The person may be unpleasant to be around, but if asked, they would still say they are happy.

This is a subgroup of happy people called dicks. This book is not written for them. I don't like them, and I don't want to be around them. They can go live on Shithead Island and complain about the weather and be happy about it.

This book is written for people who want to better enjoy their happiness.

Born Happy

We shoot out of the womb happy. Save the initial crying after being pulled into cold and the bright lights, babies and toddlers all bounce around in a pretty jovial state. Everything is new and interesting and fun.

Then, as we get just a little but older, life happens. Things such as how we are raised, our friends, and our successes or failures either bring out our happiest selves or obscure our happiness. When our happiness is obscured, it is as if we move through life wearing a mask, pretending to be this unhappy, insecure, anxious, angry, or depressed person. We are not *unhappy* per se; our happiness is just covered up.

In writing this book and evaluating my life, I saw the profound impact my obscured happiness had on my personality. Frankly, much of the time it made me into a dick. That understanding led me to this important lesson:

Lesson: A loss of happiness masks who we are capable of being. It brings out the worst in us and convinces us this distortion is who we are.

Caught in the cycle, we become trapped in an alternate personality. That person and all his or her ugliness is who we become.

Obscured happiness opens the door to an avalanche of shitty possibilities, causing the worst of us to escape. That flood of darkness and pain perpetuates our unhappiness, causing a repetitive cycle.

Wash, rinse, be unhappy, repeat

This fear, self-doubt and negativity were all created by our old friend — *thoughts*.

Thoughts turned me into an asshole.

"Mistakes have the power to turn you into something better than you were before."

-Brian Tracey

Much of my life, I was wearing the mask of a Class A, dyed-in-the-wool asshole. Now that my thoughts no longer run the show and my mask has been removed, that has changed. Now I'm just an ordinary asshole.

Yes, many people still think I'm an asshole. I am certain there are more to come. The difference is that I no longer care, because I know I am being the best asshole I can be. I am no longer trying to make the entire world laugh or make everyone like me. Now, if someone doesn't like me, it is genuine, because I am finally my authentic self. They think I'm a dick, and maybe I was to them. We were just never meant to be friends.

This was a seismic shift for me. Most of my life, my thoughts told me my mission was to always be the center of attention. To make people laugh at all costs.

Once I understood it was not just me making the jokes, I understood I was not being my true self. I uncovered my happiness.

Being happier helps me not constantly utter the type of stupid shit I will discuss in this chapter. I've learned to pay attention to my mistakes and to the negative thoughts that were causing me pain and causing me to act out. I've learned to give them the weight they deserved, which was none.

Of course, I slip up more than I'd like, and anger and/or sarcasm bubble up and express themselves through unfortunate words. I try not to beat myself up too badly when that occurs, and I apologize when it does. Furthermore, I understand that if you don't piss a few people off in your life, you probably have not achieved much and haven't really lived.

The Mouth that Roared

Some people respond to unhappiness by being reserved or withdrawn. Others may be overly chipper or appear stressed out. Some people may become boisterous or bossy, vindictive, vengeful, or mean.

I'm the last guy. The asshole. My absence of happiness caused me to act in ways I believed was *who I am*. This caused me to be insulting, too quick with an obnoxious remark, and often just unpleasant to be around.

My entire life, I exhibited diarrhea of the mouth disguised as humor, which meant constantly saying stupid shit and trying to make people like me by making them laugh. Far more often than not, without knowing it, I turned people off and gave them an inaccurate impression of me.

Imagine if Triumph the Insult Dog got Don Rickles pregnant and my sense of humor was the baby. It was relentless. Being around me meant exposure to a verbal onslaught as my brain automatically supplied my mouth with a barrage of quick-witted, very often angry and offensive comments or insults. The results were not pretty.

I consistently put my foot in my mouth, talked too much and pissed off people or offended them.

That's just who I am, I would think. ***I can't help it.***

Think about the irony. I was someone who wanted friends but did everything he could to piss people off and push them away. All of it was born out of not ever being my true self.

People's responses to interactions with me repelled them further, making it worse. My negative interactions fueled further unhappiness. It was my own personal circle of hell and I had no clue I was in it, much less how to get out. How did that happen?

The How

My journey into the psych ward was born of wanting to please the people who loved me the most — my mom and dad. They were great, loving parents. I am grateful for their advice, however misguided some of it was. Actually, it almost killed me, but I guess we all make mistakes.

As with most parents and children, part of their guidance was teaching appropriate interpersonal interactions. I should have not paid quite so much attention to my dad on that one.

Dr. Feelgood

I looked up to my dad. Despite his anxiety and his occasionally caustic demeanor, he was a great, loving man. He never missed an opportunity to tell us he loved us, give us a hug or brag about us to his friends. There was a universe of patients who adored him and who, to this day, still take time to tell my mom how much they miss him. My brothers and I would see how people looked to him for advice and laughter. At his core, Dad was a very caring guy. He just didn't always understand boundaries.

Dad was masterful with a story or a joke. When he was in the mood to tell a story, it was a treat. I studied how he told jokes and how he comported himself. I wanted to make everyone laugh, as well. I especially wanted to make him laugh, which I was often able to do, for the most part because I copied his sense of humor.

The complicated part about my dad was that his brand of humor often took a left turn and his interactions could, in the name of humor, be abrasive. I cannot say exactly where that came from. I know he grew up poor and that his dad was hard on him, sometimes physically. My mom claims that losing his hair in his early twenties made him very self-conscious as well, which he masked with humor. Looking back, it's clear to me he had some mental baggage (and baldness), both of which he passed on to me.

In his quest for a laugh, George occasionally stepped over the line--sometimes in a big way.

> *Dad was examining a patient who also happened to be a friend. As part of this annual physical, dad performed a routine prostate exam, which meant inserting a finger into the man's rectum. This exam is unpleasant enough without humor also being inserted.*
>
> *As he was knuckle deep in his patient's anus, dad thought it would be a good idea to whisper into the ear of his patient, "I've always loved you."*

The gentleman abruptly ended the exam and exited the office never to return. Nor did he ever again speak to my father.

Reading that story, your reaction is to simultaneously laugh and cringe. That is the story of my life.

On reflection and comparison to my life, I now understand my dad's gruff demeanor. In my case, I was lucky enough to realize it and change course.

Dad

The apple doesn't Fall Far

As I said, I looked up to my dad and wanted to be like him. I wanted to be a really funny guy like George.

> *Sitting next to my boss at dinner one night after a company softball game, somehow the subject of his personal office bathroom was raised. I leaned in and said in a loud whisper:*
>
> *"Hey, Have you ever gone in there in the middle of the day and tossed one off?"*

Fortunately, this was well before the human resources-heavy, millennial-driven world where it is considered a felony to say or do anything that might even remotely make anyone feel uncomfortable. Thus, I was not terminated for this. Today I would be shown the door mid-insult ... and rightly so.

> *Before the invention of e-mail and instant messaging, our beloved, "seasoned"* [7] *office receptionist was in charge of the front desk.*
>
> *Part of her job was paging people over the intercom as clients arrived. I always tried to fool her into paging a fake dirty name, but she was on to me. She could not, however, avoid going to the bathroom.*
>
> *One day I heard the voice of the new, young, inexperienced replacement receptionist over the intercom and immediately ran into the nearby conference room.*
>
> *Thirty seconds later the entire office hears her page Mike Hunt.*

I didn't understand how my words and actions had defined the way people saw me. Who did they meet? Was I the educated, witty guy I believed I was, or was I just the asshole they had the misfortune to stand next to at a meeting or a party?

Or was I both?

> *I was at a party, chatting with someone I had just met. At the end of the conversation he said to me,*

---

[7] Old

"Wow. I always heard you were an asshole. You're actually a nice guy."

Making people laugh temporarily made me feel good. Some people use alcohol. Some have drugs or sex. For me, it was laughter at any expense.

Split Personality

My entire life, I had two personalities. My first personality was deeply sensitive, tortured, contemplative, and caring — a me who only wants to offer sage wisdom, advice and love.

The second wanted to make fun of the first.

Me and James Dean. Visiting Karin in College.
Williamstown, Ma. Circa 1988

I didn't understand it, but at my core, like my dad, I was a lot more caring than asshole. I could never see it because my happiness was obscured, so I didn't show it to others.

I'd been unhappy for a long time. This made me angry, and that anger showed itself through my cutting humor and remarks. As time went on, with each verbal misstep, my embarrassment heightened.

Well into our marriage, Karin and I would leave a social gathering and she'd gently point out something I should not have said. The more that sort of thing happened, the more I wanted to crawl under a rock.

What Changed

My mentor Steve D' Annunzio hosted retreats for his students in upstate New York. The retreats provided opportunities to unplug, meditate, try yoga, and for me, insult people.

The gatherings were attended by many different types of people from various jobs, all looking to improve themselves both in business and in life. There were a wide variety of personalities. As in most situations in life, with perhaps the exception of a Klan rally, a few more shall we say *delicate folks* would attend the retreat.

When we broke into individual groups for discussion, I was being my usual aggressive self as I expressed my opinion. A woman in my group walked away and burst into tears.

Shoot! Score!

Now, in fairness to me, this woman likely cried when she took a dump, so this was no one-off for her. Nonetheless, I felt like a total asshole. Again.

Not long after that retreat, I had a coaching session with Steve where we discussed that incident. I expressed my growing frustration with my big mouth and Steve said something to me that made more sense than almost anything I'd ever heard. It was so logical yet so simple I was surprised I had not figured it out on my own. Steve said,

Lesson: Every time a mistake is repeated, it becomes more painful.

Fuck me.

That had literally been the story of my life. I was constantly being left out of events because people were simply tired of being around me, and then I felt slighted because I didn't understand why it had occurred.

Looking back, I realized this had been a pattern in my life.

> *After graduating high school, several close friends went backpacking through Europe without asking me, which stung. Then, going into my junior year of college, my three suitemates decided to move into off-campus housing and didn't ask me to join them. That was borderline devastating. Finally, at work, my constant inappropriate comments scared them enough to simply exclude me from major organizational changes.*

The moment Steve explained the *repeat mistake principle*, I was speechless. He had described my life.

My mind was spinning as I acknowledged this reality. I was overwhelmed. I felt like that clueless schmuck in *The Emperor's New Clothes*. I'd operated in a world where people often laughed "with" me, which I'd taken as encouragement, while they were secretly shocked by the things I said, resulting in a less than flattering impression of me.

I had no idea of the damage I'd caused myself. I had no idea this was all contributing to not experiencing more happiness in my life. I never took a moment to understand why I did what I did and how it impacted me. I just assumed *that's who I am* and kept repeating the pattern. I had ignored the actual reason I behaved that way.

The *why*.

Then I let the bad stuff cover up my true self.

Don't Feel Bad for Rob

You'll be happy to know in the above examples, everything had a happy ending.

Those high school friends all contracted malaria and herpes, my college roommates' house was burglarized, and the firm where I worked went bankrupt.

In reality, those high school friends are my closest buddies (the Potluck crew) and we've travelled and spent time lots of time together over the last 30 years. We've discussed the Europe thing (actually, I never miss a chance to remind them) and the fact is, if I were them, I probably wouldn't have asked me to come, either.

As for college, I actually found a really cool place to live for the first semester in the arts and music section of Albany, away from everyone, which was a great way to reset. The next semester, my former suitemates asked me to move in and, despite my reservations, it worked out pretty well. I still think it was a really fucking shitty thing to do, but I guess I earned it.

Finally, at work, I ultimately have thrived there and was recently promoted.

As I said, I have two distinct personalities. When the kinder, more thoughtful, less prone to diarrhea of the mouth personality was able to emerge, good things happened because I was at my happiest.

THE SOLUTIONS

**"Learn from yesterday, live for today,
hope for tomorrow.
The important thing is not to stop questioning."**

-Albert Einstein

W hen I shared my idea for a book with friends, they asked, "So what's the solution? What do you think the secret is to happiness?"

After much deliberation I replied, "I have no fucking clue."

While the occasional lucky bastard is born with a greater degree of happiness or a person reads a book or attends a seminar that changes the course of his or her life, in my case, uncovering happiness was more about the journey to get there than the answer to the problem.

There doesn't seem to be one specific idea, thing, or timeframe that by itself uncovered happiness for me. Throughout this adventure, I have adopted several means to interpret my thoughts and a multitude of ways to keep my happiness uncovered. These are the concepts that work well for me.

"Attachment leads to Jealousy.
The shadow of greed, that is.
Train yourself to let go of everything you fear to lose."

-Yoda

As previously discussed, attachment to an outcome or result or material thing was a real problem for me. It was probably the biggest hindrance to my experiencing happiness, so I will start there.

I have boiled down my journey towards becoming unattached below. Hopefully, it will help you avoid some of the pain I inflicted on myself.

Rob's Process for Unattaching

Step One: Understanding Need versus Want

Step One is understanding the difference between a need and a want. They are both easy concepts, yet they complicate the crap out of life when we confuse them.

Need

Need is easy because it is basic. There are virtually no *needs* beyond basic needs for food, clothing and shelter. Some poor unfortunates cannot even afford shelter and yet survive, so that one is arguable as well, depending on where you live.

When you have only your basic needs, it is possible to be at your happiest. It may not be easy, but it is possible. Need equals true *must have*.

Want

Want is everything else. Wants are desires, not necessities. Fulfilling a want provides satisfaction, not happiness.

Whether you want to buy a boat or to pass the bar exam or to go on vacation, the euphoric emotion you feel if that want is filled is actually relief. You are relieved that you have this thing you desired and don't have to think about that thing anymore.

> *When we purchased our current home, I was proud of what Karin and I had accomplished. We moved into a large, almost brand-new house in a development I loved. This had been a primary goal for me.*
>
> *Not long afterward, I ran into a somewhat obnoxious woman from our old neighborhood at the Home Depot. She greeted me with, "So, are you happy now in your big house?"*

After thinking she was a dick, I simply replied, "I was already happy. Now I just have a bigger house." Then I walked away.

That moment, worthy of a mic drop, was an excellent example of need versus want. I very much wanted a bigger house, so when we purchased it, I felt relief that I no longer needed to think about it and was satisfied we had achieved our goal. The house itself, however, could not be the source of my happiness.

Again, happiness has nothing to do with a *want to have.*

In a perfect world, isn't it better to be *good with* whatever occurs because most things are transitive? To quote Sheryl Crowe, "It's not getting what you want, it's wanting what you've got."

Step Two: Understanding Satisfaction versus Happiness

Part of becoming unattached is appreciating the difference between satisfaction, which is the feeling attachment provides when things go well, and happiness, which can be constant in all circumstances.

From passing grades, to paychecks, to sex, satisfaction is not happiness. If you define happiness by benchmarks such as cars, vacations, bonuses at work or passing a class, you are attached to something that can merely provide satisfaction.

Toward the end of 2017, I was close to achieving a milestone goal at work. Achieving this particular goal was a big deal. It meant my level of success placed me amongst the top achievers nationwide. I was certain that attaining this particular level would make me incredibly happy.

It was going to be close. In fact I wouldn't know until the very last day of the work year if I would be able to do it. The stress was driving me and every one around me nuts. I kept grinding and grinding and then...I made it by the skin of my teeth. Close or not, I was successful.

I felt great — for like a minute. Then I starting thinking about what I needed to do the next year and the shit started all over again.

In fact, at the firm-wide meeting one month later where they honored the few of us in this elite group, I was so wrapped up in whatever thr current problem was that I took no enjoyment in that celebration. My mind was somewhere else completely. The thing I had worked so hard for was done, and it had not increased my happiness one bit. What a waste.

Step Three: Controlling the Controllables

Another reason why attachment is a zero sum game is because in most cases you cannot control the thing to which you are attached.

If you are waiting on a grade, for a package to arrive, or for your favorite team to win, you have attached your feelings to something out of your control. Of course, there are things you can do to encourage the result you want (study hard, write a threatening letter to Amazon, choose a winning team for which to root) but ultimately, much of what we want is out of our control.

Step Four: Adopting Perspective

Easier Said Than Done

Understanding attachment, while helpful, is not a solution by itself. Internalizing and practicing it can be a bitch. Becoming unattached is counterintuitive. Losing a big job or commision or a game all suck and may feel crappy.

To overcome attachment, we need to dig much deeper to learn what to do when things don't go as planned. I still occasionally have to remind myself about that lesson.

The Big Picture

One way to adopt perspective is to look at your "loss" or "failure" in relationship to *the big picture.*

When you think about the simple notion of how small anyone's wants, needs, or problems are, you add perspective and lessen the significance of anything to which you are attached. The world has been turning for billions of years, and it will keep doing so long after we are gone. Whatever outcome seems so important to us now is not even a pimple on an elephant's ass in the grand scheme of our lives, let alone the universe.

I recognize that when things go bad you may want to wallow in it a bit. Many has been the time a person has said to me, "Life goes on," and I just wanted to kick them in the balls.

Yet, they were right. Those are the truest three words in the world.

LIFE. GOES. ON.

Until it doesn't. Then you are dead, and who gives a fuck that you didn't pass a test?

Winning a game, getting a poor grade, being turned down for a loan, purchasing a car or a house, or receiving or not receiving a promotion are all significant events, but they don't define you. Those outcomes can only affect your temporary satisfaction, not your happiness.

I try to remember that all things in life, indeed life itself, are transitive, so there is no reason to become attached to them.

Step Five: Surrender

This is the ability to release your feelings about a result (e.g., attachment). It is the most important step and therefore is discussed in greater detail in its own chapter.

The short version is that unattaching is really hard and you may need an actual tool to do it. That tool is surrender. Stay tuned…

Conclusion

There is no reason for me to reinvent the wheel for this chapter's lesson. Humans have been struggling with attachment for quite some time. Much has been written on the subject of attachment by women and men far smarter, wiser, and deader than me.

The conclusion they have all reached is that so long as you are *attached* or *connected* to an outcome — whether positive or negative — you have taken your happiness out of your hands.

"It is the mark of an educated mind to be able to entertain a thought without accepting it."

-Aristotle

"The clinging to desire comes from our experience of short-term satisfaction. We ignore the fact that satisfying our desires doesn't bring an end to them."

-Buddha. The Second Noble Truth

"The principle cause of suffering is the attachment to 'desire' or 'craving.' Both desire to have (wanting) and desire not to have (aversion)."

-Unknown

In other words, get over it.

"Surrender, surrender, but don't give yourself away."

-Cheap Trick

Fear and Surrender

The root of negative thinking is fear. When we worry or feel stress or anxiety, it is based on our fear of an action or event. I call this the *what if syndrome.*

"What if I fail?"

"What if she doesn't call me back?"

"What if I don't get that raise?"

The list is literally endless.

As a naturally negative person, I am envious of those who can put a positive spin on things. Naturally positive (or better, perhaps, naturally fearless) people appear to disregard fear and instead either do not entertain any other outcome or will ask the opposite question. They wonder, "Wouldn't it be great if I get the part in the show?" Or, "Maybe they will ask me out." It seems naturally fearless

167

people innately understand how to disregard negative thoughts. This is a form of surrender, which is accepting a thing, a thought, or an idea while simultaneously denying it your energy.

When your brain is defensively wired, as mine is, you are susceptible to fear-based thinking, which makes surrender extremely challenging. I was programmed by my upbringing to consider the worst, give my thoughts energy, and make life harder on myself and those around me. I had to learn surrender.

The Art of Surrender

What is Surrender?

Surrender is applied by people in different ways as a defense against negativity or unfavorable circumstances. This is not a definitive guide to surrender. It is just how I learned to apply it.

Surrender is a strategy of accepting that particular thoughts are happening, denying them your mental energy and allowing the thoughts to occur without assigning them a value. This is not the same as denying the existence of the thought itself, which you cannot do. If you can find a method to avoid providing negative thoughts meaning, such as replacing them with positive thoughts, you are practicing a form of surrender.

Negative thoughts tap into our worries and concerns. We cannot help that. They feed on fear. The more fear we experience, the more rapidly negativity is generated until we cannot control it.

When I was unaware of the art of surrender, I was angry, stressed, anxious and resentful.[8] Those negative feelings, which felt as if they took no effort to achieve because they happened automatically, actually used up all my energy. They were so demanding that I had nothing left with which to fight back. I gave into negativity, which made happiness impossible.

How to Learn to Practice Surrender

Step 1 - The Origin of Negative Thought

The first step in practicing surrender is understanding the origin of our negative thoughts.

The basis of negative thought is fear. You energize your fear by believing or validating it. This gives birth to your negative thought, which builds on itself, and then your brain is off to the races. You defeat yourself before the thing you are worried about even has a chance to occur.

Step 2 — Understanding Fear

The second step I took toward surrender was breaking down fear. Fear is composed of fables (some call them lies) we convince ourselves to be true. To remember this idea, I

---

[8] We are all imperfect. I can be a real dick sometimes, but far less often now.

use the acronym F.E.A.R. as a reminder. The definition of fear is:

F alse

E vidence

A ppearing

R eal

Although I generally think acronyms aren't helpful, and are in fact awful, when someone explained F.E.A.R. to me, it stuck. If you can accept that F.E.A.R. under-LIES (false evidence) negative thought, surrender isn't far behind. If you give into your fear, bad things inevitably occur.

From 2010-2012 I had a personal assistant. During our period of time working together, I felt comfortable enough around her to be myself. The problem is that what I was willing to say when I was comfortable was far different than with many other people.

Unbeknownst to me during those two years, from day one, my assistant kept a running list of things everyone within her earshot said that offended her delicate sensibilities. Those things often emanated from me. The list was long, although in my defense, the stuff she didn't make up was some of my best work.

To be crystal clear, since I know what you are thinking, nothing I said was directed at or was about her in an inappropriate sexual way. Let's just say that if I was going to do that, she was not my type.

Realizing her tenure with me was coming to an end, she of course hired a fucking lawyer, who mailed a letter to my boss threatening to sue.

Without getting into the merits and what actually occurred, all I will say is that three months and tens of thousands of dollars later it was over and settled. I learned a painful lesson and it was done. For no particular reason, one of my fears had always been a lawsuit.

It had happened. The other shoe had dropped, and I was still standing.

My thoughts had other ideas. Although it was done, I descended into a psychological tailspin. In addition to feeling angry and unable to forgive myself, I felt my trust had been violated. I became despondent and could barely work.

My thoughts became irrational. Every thought centered around my fear. What complaints and lawsuits were lurking in the dark, waiting to be thrown at me? My career was over. I would be stripped of my licenses. I felt helpless and I remember thinking, "I cannot believe I am in this situation. It is 1995 all over again."

Of course, it wasn't even close to the circumstances of 1995. It was an isolated, solvable incident which I had the wherewithal to overcome. Nonetheless, my thoughts took over, and I gave them all the energy they demanded. I believed the lies. I gave into fear by believing all the *what ifs*.

Step 3 - Withholding Energy

The final step for practicing surrender is to withhold energy from your fear-based thoughts. When we refuse to energize our negative thoughts, they shrivel and die or float away. This one may take a bit more explanation.

The concept of withholding energy from a thought may sound stupid to you. Frankly, it sounds stupid to me. If it makes you feel less earthy-crunchy, substitute "withholding energy" for "punching a thought in the face." Whatever phrase you use, it works.

In *The Power of Now*, Eckhardt Tolle explained, *"If you find your here and now intolerable and it makes you unhappy, you have three options:*

- *reject it (remove yourself from the situation)*
- *change it, or*
- *totally accept it"*

As he further explained, the one option you do not have is to deny or resist it.

This concept applies to thought. When you resist a negative thought, it wins, because you are giving it attention and therefore devoting mental energy to it. You have allowed it to distract you.

Accepting a thought means accepting its *existence*, not its truth. Therefore, rather than denying a thought, change how you treat it. You can accept all your thoughts but only give your energy (attention) to the positive ones. If your thought is negative, acknowledge it and let it float away. When negative thoughts occur, effortlessly say, "Thank you," and immediately surrender them to the universe or God or Buddha or Jesus or Krishna or the trash if you are an atheist.

**"The only thing that holds true happiness
is that moment when you're in it.
Nothing can be controlled."**

-Eliza Doolittle

I primarily live without regrets. Living in the past, regretting what you should or should not have done is a waste of time. It takes away from your now.

Staying out of the past is not possible, however, when you write a book about yourself. You are forced back into all the parts of your life, both good and bad. That leads to rethinking how you lived those parts and what you might have done differently.

I already discussed the miscarriage, which I did not handle well. The other big regret relating directly to my happiness is not devoting the proper amount of time and effort after my suicide attempt to understanding what I'd done and why I'd done it. Had I spent time and been more thoughtful, I would have known what I was looking for as I "searched for happiness." Had I looked for a definition of happiness, I would have found it much sooner. I would not have tortured myself and Karin with my stress and worry.

Life is a Marathon, Not a Sprint

My rush back to into a "normal" life was understandable. Once out of the hospital, I was so relieved to be done with law that I convinced myself that my breakdown was because of a bad career choice and not faulty wiring. I jumped back into the world headfirst and the results were often not pretty.

My thoughtless reentry into the world prevented me from addressing the reasons I'd gone off the rails, which was that I had no fucking idea of what happiness was supposed to look like. I dove in and for twenty-three years, I searched in the dark.

I realize the whole concept of taking time to create a definition of happiness may appear ridiculous. Who the hell wastes time coming up with a definition of happiness? If you ask most people for an actual definition of happiness, they'll struggle to find an answer and call you an asshole. It's not something our parents taught us. You were just expected to put a smile on your face and *be happy*.

In hindsight, if I'd had some kind of psychic anchor — in this case, a definition of happiness, something to remember when things got rough and to guide me daily — my internal battles would have been easier to overcome.

Law was a problem, but it was not THE problem. Law was external. Happiness is internal. How can you know if you are happy if you don't know what happiness feels like?

What is Happiness?

I wanted my definition to be something that could take me out of a mental spiral but would also serve as an internal beacon to follow every day. The definition needed to remind me of the things that mattered most. You might want to think of it as kind of a value statement.

The hardest part about composing a definition was that it was counterintuitive. In the abstract, I knew it should have nothing to do with having things or achieving goals, other than the goal of happiness. My problem was that I am wired for achievement.[9] To be clear, that is not always a positive and doesn't always mean I achieve everything to which I set my mind. That is what led me to my overdose. I set my mind on achievement in law and when that became emotionally impossible, I short-circuited. Therefore, the idea that the most important things in life are not goal-oriented was foreign to me.

I'd always had a fear of failure. Sales is an inherently achievement-oriented business. If you polled anyone with whom I work, they would confirm their belief that to stop worrying about the next piece of business or what action a prospect was going to take would be setting yourself up for failure. To worry, in other words to cover up happiness, is what we all feel makes us successful. That relates to the seperate topic of surrender as discussed in the last chapter.

Dancing with Myself

---

[9] My daughters call that statement a "humble brag." I tell them to fuck off.

In the abstract, I knew happiness should have nothing to do with what people own or how much money they make, where they live or what vacations they take. Yet in the Type-A, results-driven world many of us inhabit, I'd experience positive feelings when mine and Karin's successes allowed us to provide nice things for our family.

No one would look at me funny if I said, "Taking my family on a vacation to Bermuda makes me happy." Taken in this context, it seems like taking pride in your accomplishments should be part of happiness.

It is not.

The logic is flawed because feelings such as pride, while important, are impermanent. You may be proud of your ability to provide and then lose your job and go bankrupt. You may still feel proud of what you accomplished in the past, but it doesn't stop you from feeling like shit now.

If you used the definition above, your happiness is gone. The ups and downs of life engender only temporary emotions. Passing a test, getting your driver's license, or landing a job all cause us to feel good, but the feelings always pass. I have done all those things and my feelings about them now, if I even have any, are neutral. The pleasure I felt at the time they happened was satisfaction, which is temporary.

The Journey

I had no specific strategy for composing a definition of happiness. I simply started thinking about it as I read books and contemplated the meaning of life and happiness.

I didn't focus at all on material goals or even important personal goals such as health, which are transitive and cannot ultimately be controlled by me. I considered what things brought me *peace* as opposed to *joy*. I asked myself, "What are the things that give me perspective or make me feel *centered*?"

During this exercise, I ran across the following quote:

"Happiness is a journey, not a destination."

I had seen this quote many times before without its importance registering. I was always in such a hurry, wrapped up in my own head. It was one of those sayings that looked good on a poster but seemed impossible in practice. If I have to bust my ass to earn something (a.k.a. the journey), I was always happiest with the *getting it* part (a.k.a. the destination).

This time, the quote resonated. I guess after suffering so long with stress, my defenses were down against things that would help me. I was exhausted and willing to listen to anything. I accepted this wisdom and it turned out to be the kickstart I needed to compose my own definition of happiness. I was finally willing to surrender my fear of failure.

But Just What the Hell did that Quote Mean?

As I considered that quote, it occurred to me that if happiness was the journey, it must be something that always existed. We were always on a journey somewhere. Life itself is simply a journey between birth and death, isn't it?

Pondering this question, my own jewel of wisdom popped into my brain:

Happiness represents a state of being, not a state of having.

I thought I was a fucking genius coming up with that one!

For about one minute, anyway.

A quick Google search revealed that pretty much every Buddhist scholar, monk, and/or citizen of Tibet has said this or something like it. It may even be the first thing they say to each other in the morning as a greeting. It was not even *slightly* original.

On the other hand, that idea itself was completely original to *me*, which is what I believe was vital.

I had to realize it on my own.

Rob's Definition of Happiness

Armed with my new quote, I was ready to expand it into a full-blown definition. I wanted my happiness to be consistent, so I knew my definition had to represent something I could feel in all situations, both positive and negative, having nothing to do with money, things or even health. I wanted to feel it all the time, every day, up until I took my last breath.

My definition needed to rely only on my mind. It could **only** be achieved internally, within me. Theoretically, anything can occur outwardly in my life and my happiness does not change.

It is a lifetime goal that won't always be easy to see, but in my heart, it will always be there for me.

This is my definition of happiness:

Happiness is a consistent feeling of appreciation and gratitude. It is peaceful, not aggressive, and loving without trying. In happiness, things that don't go my way don't bother me, and things that go my way don't sway me. Happiness exists when I get nothing I want. I can experience happiness on a day everything goes wrong. I can be in a bad mood and still be happy. My enjoyment and appreciation of happiness is the result of how I interpret my life up to that moment.

You may not appreciate my overly wordy definition of happiness. You may view a definition as a crutch.

I prefer to view it as a defense against the most powerful thing in the world — our minds. Everything we say and do is controlled by the currency of our minds —*thought*. Thought can be our greatest friend, but it is often our most dangerous enemy. Whatever mechanisms we develop to handle the power of our minds, we will experience more happiness when we make use of them.

"Own Your Shit!"

-Rob Segall

**""The fault, dear Brutus, is not in our stars,
But in ourselves..."**

-Bill Shakespeare

Fucking Lawyers

You may have deduced by now that I don't hold the legal profession in particularly high esteem. I came by my feelings honestly, having been exposed to their bullshit well before entering practice.

I knew early on that I had a problem with the approach lawyers take toward the concept of blame, which is the profession's stock in trade. I was particularly repulsed by plaintiff's personal injury attorneys, which happened to be my oldest brother's chosen line of work. Before I even entered law school, he would regale us at family dinners with descriptions of "great" injury cases and the utter bullshit claims from which they arose. It bothered me to

183

no end. One thing I knew for certain was that I would not be chasing ambulances.

Deflection of responsibility is something upon which modern-day law, and indeed modern-day thought, focuses. No one ever just slips anymore or is injured just because they are careless. No one enters into a crappy contract anymore just because they are bad dealmakers. Someone always screwed us, hurt us, or took advantage of us. We must sue them. The blame game is now our default.

In fairness to both lawyers and legitimate claimants, blame can be necessary and we need lawers to lead the charge. Without lawyers, how would victims of alleged predators (for example, people whose names rhyme with Harvey Weinstein and Jeffrey Epstein) seek justice? The same goes for defective product lawsuits. Those are examples of when blame is necessary and effective because the victims have no other recourse. There is no deflection of responsibility because those victims were exploited.

There are also civil rights lawyers, contract lawyers, intellectual property lawyers, real estate lawyers, etc., who all have a place in this world.

I am talking about the 95% of other lawyers.

In any event, I think much of law represents denial of accountability, and that is just a reflection of much of society today. If you can never own your shit, you will never be happy.

Why Blame is Bad

Blame feels easy when things go to shit. Eschewing blame takes almost no effort. Deflecting fault to a person or a circumstance for our problems seems less painful than owning up to our situation.

After the blaming is done, however, has it made your situation any better? Casting blame only frustrated me, pissed me off and usually upset the target of my blame — my parents. It never made me feel happier. In fact, it made me feel powerless, because after I exhausted myself with anger, nothing changed, and I remained in the same frustrating situation. I'd exerted all this energy in an attempt to make myself temporarily feel better and ended up feeling worse. It prevented me from taking full responsibility for my life and for achieving happiness.

Even when someone or something else is 100% at fault for your problem, as you blame them, ask yourself, "How is this helping me?"

A few years back, a friend asked me a great question when I was frustrated by a situation I felt was *not my fault*. I wanted the person on the other side of the dispute to admit their culpability in the matter to assuage my anger. It turned into an argument and I was pissed off.

My friend, offering some excellent advice, asked me the following question:

Lesson: Would you rather be happy, or right?

We need to accept that oftentimes we cannot be both.

Of course, there will be times you are wronged or damaged and the offender can/should make amends, and you should look to them for a solution. I'm not advocating taking the blame for something you didn't do.

What I am saying is that most times casting blame does nothing to help a situation. When you stop trying to convince everyone you are right, you immediately save a bunch of negative energy.

Admittedly, this doesn't always work. Some people instinctively want to be angry and cast blame, so there have even been times I immediately owned something and yet the aggrieved party kept yelling at me. At that point, I had to tell them to shut the fuck up. But that is another chapter.

The Parent Trap

That may be true but...

Like many people, I fell into the blame trap. I spent many years being angry at my parents. I blamed them for my shitty career choice, my depression, and my eventual short circuit.

I was a victim of the blaming mentality for many years. This hindered my happiness until I took stock of my own 'responsibility for my life. In fairness, part of the reason I held onto my anger was my parents' initial refusal to accept they had any part in my meltdown. Maybe out of their own fear or guilt or whatever, their first reaction toward me was anger.

I blamed them for "forcing me" into law and causing my breakdown. They were the easy and obvious targets. Blaming them, however, didn't make me any happier or make my life any better. Furthermore, it was bullshit.

Yes, my parents had lead roles in my personal drama. They were the primary reason I went to law school, which led to some bad stuff. That said, even if every bad thing that ever happened to me was their fault, in the end, who cares? At some point I needed to stop whining and move on.

I had already taken control of my professional life and was succeeding. Everything before that was history, so being upset with them ultimately accomplished absolutely NOTHING.

It wasn't until I let go of blame and saw my own culpability that I could truly begin helping myself. Then I could accept that the responsibility for fixing me was all on me.

It's true that passing on ideas, worries, aspirations and dreams to children can have a big impact on their thought processes and the direction of their lives. I am of the opinion that many parents are not mindful enough of the impact their advice holds. From that perspective, my parents made mistakes.

What is always overlooked by assholes like me, however, is that **they are only human.** They did their best. What more can you ask than for someone to do their best?

Everything my parents did came from love. What they passed on also helped me achieve the success I have had in my life.

For years, I blamed my parents for my overdose, until I realized the same people who "caused" my breakdown instilled the values that later allowed me to turn my life around. It was patently unfair of me to assign all the blame and none of the credit. Having my own family caused me to understand the tremendous challenges of parenting and allowed me to develop a much deeper understanding of the love and selflessness that backed up their guidance, as well as the intense pain they felt watching me suffer.

Karin

Looking back at the immediate aftermath of my overdose was instructive on the topic of blame. Karin had every reason to blame me for the shit situation in which she found herself. She had nothing to do with my overdose. She could easily have left. We had no kids, and she had a good job. She was angry and scared. And I'd totally checked out. Before this event occurred, I was a shaking, weepy, nonfunctioning mess. I was willing to die and leave her alone to pick up the pieces. A portion of the income in our home was now just gone.

She stayed by my side despite my worries and a life suddenly filled with uncertainty. I didn't consider it at the time, but as overwhelmed and fed up as she was, Karin never stopped loving me, and even if she felt it, she never told me she blamed me. There are times even now that I cannot believe anyone could love me enough to put up with what I had put her through. I didn't have the capacity at that time to understand the impact my actions had on her.

More than anything…*she never blamed me.*

Karin's actions in the wake of my suicide attempt taught me as much about how to handle blame as it did about the depth of love. She handled it like a rock star. That is something I'll never forget.

Apple Picking, Cortland Manor, New York 2015

Chapter 21: Be Yourself
(but learn from your mistakes, dummy)

"Be yourself.
Everyone else is already taken."

-Oscar Wilde

I do a pretty good job of beating myself up about my mouth. I feel thankful, nonetheless, for my sense of humor.

Laughter is one of the greatest joys in my life. Being funny provides far more positives than negatives. Making people laugh brings me happiness. I love seeing people smile. I love how it lightens the mood in a room. Humor can take a bite out of sadness in situations.

On February 22, 2004, my phone rang at 4:00 a.m. It was Mom calling to tell me Dad had passed away during the night. He had been ill with pancreatic cancer and had recently taken a turn for the worse, so we knew this day was imminent. I called my brothers and cousins and began the emotional trip over to my parents' home.

I came into the house and walked upstairs into my parents' room. There, sitting in the room, were my mom, my brothers, my cousins, and a family friend who'd been staying with my mom. In the corner was my deceased father, lying in a hospital bed my parents had put in the room for him, quiet and still. I looked at his body and then at the assemblage of people in the room, back at Dad and then back at the people. I was surprised no one had covered him up, although looking back, I guess that act was just too final for them.

In that moment, however, I found the whole scene morbidly funny.

They were all sitting there, talking in a whisper right next to my dad. So, I walked in and said,

"Hey Mom, hey Dad, how's everybody doing?" Everybody cracked up.

My joke didn't mean I didn't love Dad or that I was being disrespectful. My father would have laughed his huge stomach attached to a skinny butt off. It lifted heaviness out of the room, if only for a moment. In that instance, laughter was love.

Sometimes humor breaks the ice, and those are times I enjoy:

A CPA invited me and a member of my asset management team to his office for an interview. He was considering having us manage money for one of his clients. This required moving it away from the current advisor, whom I did not know. My teammate didn't know the CPA.

As we began chatting, I asked the CPA the other advisor's name. When told me, I immediately replied,

"Oh, it's great that he's out of jail."

The CPA looked at me quizzically and then burst out laughing. He also gave us the business.

The problem with my humor had always been the velocity of my mouth. My brain works lightning fast trying to get a laugh. I reflexively search for *funny* in every situation, with the process often occurring too quickly to stop. A comment bullies its way past the censor in my brain and then my mouth grabs it and spits it out.

I was introduced to a new financial planning client. She closed the door to her office and said,

"Before we work together, it's important for you to know that I'm a lesbian.

"Really?" I replied. "What part of Lesbia are you from?"

This was my pattern. I said something equally funny and inappropriate, whether at work or amongst a group of friends, believing laughter was the most important thing. A few hours or days later I had to deal with the consequences.

It contributed greatly to my own underlying uneasiness and anxiety, which only served to make me try even harder.

I maintain that despite my sense of humor, I am inherently a kind person and the purpose of my humor is not to cause harm. Testament to that is the number of people who have become good friends despite their first impression of me. I like to joke that the phrase I most often hear is, "Wow, I heard you are a dick, but you are actually a good guy."

The secret was to figure out how to occasionally skip over the "you're a dick" part.

Lesson Learned?

Going back to an earlier chapter, I was caught in a downward spiral. I wasn't happy, which obscured who I could be. That caused me to try even harder for laughs to feel good about myself, pissing off more people and making me increasingly feel like crap, covering up even more happiness.

As time progressed, each time I upset someone with words, I felt significantly more horrible. It made me feel small. More than once I vowed to just clam up altogether, only to slip up time and again. That was like saying I'd stop breathing.

Complicating things, mine are not your typical slip-ups. My slip-ups are epic. When I drop a dumb comment it generally nukes the place. I have gone a year without a problem and then absolutely blown up a situation with one thoughtless comment.

Then I feel even worse.

Lesson Learned!

The turning point for me occurred in 2012, when I once again made a regrettable joke to a colleague in the hallway at work. In what I thought was a whisper, I said to the colleague/friend,

> *"Hey Jon, if you let me work this case by myself, I'll let you sleep with my wife."*

The off-color joke was overheard by a young employee sitting within earshot. Of course, it wasn't meant for her to hear but that is beside the point. She reported it to human resources, and I was called in for a discussion.

I couldn't believe I had done it again. I had been trying so hard and yet my carelessness was again my enemy.

Sitting across from Michael Book, the head of our firm, in his office, I turned my head so he couldn't see the tears welling up in my eyes as embarrassment overtook me. It was particularly bad because I had known Michael eighteen years, and considered him a friend whom I respected and greatly admired. I was expecting the worst.

His reaction surprised me.

He said, "Rob, you are a funny person, and you have to be who you are. It is what makes you Rob Segall. Just calm it down. Think first."

I thought this was extremely generous of him, especially since I'd expected anger. I was angry enough at myself for both of us.

From that point forward, I was mostly a model citizen. I wish I could say I have not slipped up again, but at least I can say that I have been far better and improve every day.

> *In 2017, a new colleague named David joined the firm. We passed each other in the hall many times, occasionally chatted and became friendly. One day we decided to go to lunch and I felt more comfortable being me.*

> *At the end of the lunch he said to me, "In the entire time I have been here I don't think I have ever seen you smile. You are really funny."*

I took that as both a major victory — and, I suppose, a bit of a defeat. It was an overcorrection by me, but I can say on balance, staying out of trouble makes me enjoy more happiness. I just needed to do a better job picking my spots.

As it relates to happiness, there are two lessons that apply here. The first is,

Lesson: The pain of regret hurts far more than the pain of discipline.

It was entirely possible for me to be funny in a way that was harmless and to pick my spots better. I identified that every time I insulted someone (who didn't deserve it) it detracted from my happiness.

The second is:

Lesson: Every time a lesson needs to be relearned, it becomes more painful.

I still jump on my thoughts, and my mouth is still swift and ready to react, ready to remark and ready to slay anyone in its path. The difference is that I do a better (not perfect) job of catching myself.

**"Instead, I have an abundance mentality:
When people are genuinely happy at the successes
of others, the pie gets larger."**

-Stephen Covey

Abundance is another topic where much has been written by many wise and learned people. While I have nothing particularly new to offer on the subject itself, I would like to stress how important adopting an abundance mentality is to being happy.

Abundance is easily explained by examining its opposite, known as *scarcity*. Understanding scarcity is necessary to embrace abundance, because so many of us are taught scarcity from an early age and that hinders our enjoyment of happiness.

Scarcity is a concept rooted in fear. Fear that you won't have *enough* and therefore you must deny others. In other words, someone else having something means by definition that you do not have that thing, as if they have taken it from you.

When I was in college, my friend and I were discussing panhandling, more commonly known as begging. He shared a simple philosophy he'd learned from his dad that stayed with me. While I didn't identify it as *abundance*, looking back, that is exactly what my friend was teaching me.

His dad said, "If a person comes up and asks for a dollar for something to drink (remember this was 1986 — drinks were less expensive back then), give him the dollar if you can. While it is true that he may not use it for the drink, if he is in a position where he is asking, feel some empathy for him."

There are instances throughout our lives every day where we have the option to turn left at scarcity or right at abundance.

In law school, my buddy Dave, who is far smarter than me, helped me in every class where I struggled. He didn't have to help me. It wasn't his fault I was having difficulty. Technically, it took away time from his own preparation, yet he never said "no" when asked.

When Jimmy hired me, he paid me money he could not really afford. I know how many people would have said, "I'd love to help you but…"

When I started working in financial services, my friend Larry bought a life insurance policy he absolutely did not need. He had no kids, was not married, and was starting out himself. He bought it because he loved me. Same for my lifelong friends Andy and Adam. I know I am missing several others, as well.

My mom has never once said "no" when I asked her for help, whether it be financial earlier in my adult life or otherwise. I know of many examples where this is not the case with parents. Furthermore, she is happy about every single achievement, big or small, that I, Karin or the kids have made.

In each of these examples, it is not surprising that all of these people have done well and/or are beloved in their lives. I don't think that is a coincidence. I've also found that when people practice scarcity, they often struggle.

I remember a time Karin and I were asked to dinner by an older relative who was already established in life. We were maybe just out of law school. He and his wife proceeded to order up a storm while Karin and I ordered carefully. They then insisted on splitting the bill evenly. This was a pattern with this couple who, not shockingly, eventually experienced incredible financial difficulty.

I have an acquaintance who cannot hear of someone else doing well without talking about themself and what they are doing. If they ever do anything nice for someone else, they must make sure everyone knows about it. They struggle to make friends.

Another unfortunate person is extraordinarily cheap. They become unreasonably stressed about money and have therefore made many decisions in their life to not spend money or to spend it on the wrong things because of their scarcity mentality.

Experienced advisors in my office choose to forgo an assistant or share one assistant because they don't wish to spend money. I can tell you unequivocally that refusal to share your money with excellent staff always limits your upside.

In terms of how this translates to happiness, it is simple. When you live in scarcity, you are looking inward. You are only looking at you, to yourself and how you can keep what you have. It makes you suspicious and obnoxious, and repels people. When you live abundantly, you look outward to how you can help others and thereby attract people who wish to help you.

Lesson: When you live as abundantly as possible, you get back far more than you give.

> **"Teach your children well,**
> **Your father's hell, did slowly go by.**
> **And feed them on your dreams.**
> **The one they picked. The one you'll know by."**

-Crosby, Still, Nash and Young

Parents believe they know what is "right" for their children. Realistically, that is only true for a brief time.

My siblings and I were taught to believe that our parents' guidance would lead us to the right place in life. They wanted us to feel this way.

Audrey and George loved us and felt it was their obligation to play the role of our protectors. They also were afraid, perhaps subconsciously, that we would fail on our own. For myself and my brothers, in different degrees we felt as if their advice was always right, and our problems could always be fixed with their help. This was an unwittingly dishonest portrayal of the world and caused us all pain in different ways throughout our lives.

High School Graduation. New City, New York. 1984.
I'm in the middle. Six months earlier, when I was on the brink of
failing physics my senior year, my father informed me that
if I didn't step it up, I would end up a ditchdigger.

When I decided to write this book, I thought I had everything figured out. I thought I understood how my life had unfolded. As I started to reflect and put the different pieces together, I was surprised at how little control I actually had for the first half of my life.

Talkin' About My Generation

Our parents created an atmosphere where their words mattered the most. We were unduly influenced by how they felt and what they said, so the weight of their words had more impact than it should have been.

They wanted this dynamic because it was what they knew. It was how they'd grown up. My dad was raised by immigrants who occasionally parented him in physically abusive ways. My mom had a domineering mother whose only words of advice I remember were, "It's just as easy to marry a rich one as a poor one." There was also "I've always loved Maurice (my brother) the best," which was more of a *fuck you* than advice. That's okay. I loved my Bubba Anna (my dad's mom) more than her, anyway.

Given their overbearing Jewish roots, my parents were saints. They did the best they could with the tools their parents had provided them.

My Three Sons

My brothers and I all looked up to my dad. He was a big personality. He sincerely and thoroughly loved us. That was never in question. George wanted a better life for my brothers and me than he'd had growing up and, to his credit, he and my mom accomplished that.

George was definitive in his beliefs and direct in expressing them, especially when it came to his boys. The challenge, which until now I did not understand, was that he did not comprehend the breadth of his impact on us.

His parenting method was not a constant barrage of advice drilled into us nor father/son talks about important things in life. His method was more perfectly timed comments or acts that cut right to the heart of the matter.

Cuts like a Knife

I don't want to paint an inaccurate portrait of my dad. Ninety percent of what Dad said to us was some expression of love or pride. The problem was that in the codependent atmosphere our parents had created, the negative carried a lot more weight.

Just a few words, spoken or written, could be crushing.

Albany college graduation, May 1988. It was a perfect, beautiful, sunny day. My friends and I were all excited for this moment. It was going to be a great day. Everyone was happy.

For that afternoon, with my family and my girlfriend Karin there to cheer me on, I was grateful I was able to put the notion of law school and pressure aside for the day. They had been on my mind quite a lot as the end of college loomed.

Just after the ceremony ended, with everyone feeling great and exchanging hugs, my dad walks up to me and hands me an envelope with a greeting card. This might not seem like a big deal, but in all of my 22 years, my father had never purchased a card for me. That was always Mom's department. I was pretty touched he'd gone to the trouble.

I opened the envelope, excited and curious to see what sentimental note he had written on this glorious day. Removing the card, I saw a cartoon drawing of a mouse about to reach the top of a hill, having just pushed an elephant up the entire way.

The front of the card says, "You've come a long way..." I then open it and see three more elephants at the bottom of the hill waiting to be pushed with the follow-up line, "but don't stop pushing."

That is the only thing I remember about my graduation.

Now you may think that was not such a big deal. "Don't be a pussy" may even come to mind. Perhaps you're right. From my vantage point, however, I was already heading into an unknown existence. It wasn't really one of my choosing, and the person directing me was already telling me to try harder. That message rocked my world on a day that for most people at age 21 or 22 is one of the most accomplished of their lives.

Fucking. Try. Harder.

Right?

I would argue parents have little idea what is "right" for their kids when it comes to their life's calling. How could they? Most adults I know need help conducting their own lives. Pretending they know the best career or life choice for someone else is guesswork at best and untruthful at worst, especially when motivated by a parent's fear or desire.

> *April 12, 1995. It was the day after my overdose. I was checked into the hospital and stable. My parents drove down from Rockland County to visit me. They arrived at NYU and made their way up the elevator to the 7th floor where the psych ward was located.*

As they exited the elevator, my father's pace slowed considerably, almost to a crawl. It was similar to when I'd left Karin that last time in Grand Central before the overdose.

He was afraid.

They made it into the lounge. We had our visit, both my parents and I filled with anger and fear. They departed.

Later that day, my dad spoke to my cousin Jim and said, "I guess he won't be the first Jewish president." That's what my dad was thinking about.

My parents and my dad especially, who'd grown up fairly poor, had a Depression-era mentality. They'd lived through the cold, hard reality of prolonged economic downturn. They were motivated by fear. It was extremely important to them that their children "aim high." For many of us, that meant having an advanced degree.

Mom and Dad decided that law was a good career choice for all of their children. If there had been ten of us, it still would have been the same thing. Their plan was that they would pay for law school because we would have stability as lawyers and their job would be complete, so they would not have to worry about us.

That didn't work out so well. In fact, only one of us still practices today.

My father and his three future fucking lawyers. Circa 1985.

Our entire lives, they constantly worried about us and wanted to interject their opinions into our lives. In their minds, they were providing "assistance," even when they should have allowed us to fail. Ultimately, this made their own lives much harder as they watched each of us crash and burn at different times.

By trying to direct us into our adult years, my parents took on a whole menu of unnecessary responsibilities and worries. Their fretting not only reduced their own happiness, it fucked us up as adults.

I attempted suicide. When my dad died in 2004, one of my brothers had a complete meltdown. My other brother had his own world of shit with which he had to deal.

Parents can give their children a strong foundation, but children need to build their lives on their own. We should not force help on them. Guiding a child is necessary and appropriate, but when a parent "wants" the child to follow a particular path, whose desires are they fulfilling? Wanting a child to follow a mold you've created does not always have the desired effect.

And sometimes you should just shut the fuck up.

My job at J & I Video was the opposite of glamorous. I was in jeans, sweeping floors, selling, picking up coffee for everyone (when it was my turn), and practicing a little law on occasion. I felt great.

Objectively, it was not a lifetime career move. At 30 years of age, however, I needed to do the math on that one with my wife, not my parents.

One weekend during this period Karin and I were visiting with my parents. As we were chatting over brunch, my mom slips into the discussion, in a kind of matter-of-fact but clearly premediated fashion:

"Maybe one of the executives at the studios where you buy the movies will meet you and give you a job."

Without missing a beat and without thinking, I looked at my folks and said:

"Mom. Dad. I love you. But I don't give a shit what you think of me anymore."

Mic drop. That was a turning point for me. My mother cried, having never heard that sort of thing from me, and I suppose, upset that their approval was officially no longer needed. That was the moment I really felt free of their grip for the first time.

Are You Fucking Kidding Me?

Even after moving in my own direction, my parents' words had significant influence over me.

Consider the fact that I had bounced back from a suicide attempt, reinvented myself, and was excelling in a new career. When I left *J & I*, Karin and I had virtually no money in the bank and I had a job that was commission-only with no idea if I would succeed.

Within three years, Karin and I turned everything around. You would think my parents would just be thanking god every day their son and his awesome wife, who stayed with him, were doing so well after what had occurred (and almost occurred).

It was July 2000. Karin was killing it at work. I was excelling at Cowan Financial Group. Things were going really well for us. In fact, within three years of starting my career in financial services, I was probably making close to what my father the doctor had earned in his best years.

Things were going so well Karin and I were able to sell our townhouse and purchase a larger home in Ardsley, the town where we wished to settle. We were so excited. The house was much larger than our townhouse and had a great back yard. It was super nice and we were so proud of our accomplishment.

Admittedly, the home was modest compared to my parents' home across the river in Rockland County. Unlike Westchester, Rockland was not easily commutable to New York City, so for the same amount of money we paid in Westchester, you could have three times the home and land.

Nonetheless, it was a nice home and we were excited about what we'd accomplished.

That little fact did not matter to Dad.

As he walked into the house and looked around, the first words out of his mouth were, "This is all you get for all that money?"

I was devastated.

My Parents did not Suck

This is not a blame game. George and Audrey were guilty only of love. They didn't realize the effect it had on the child they wanted to be happy.

This book is centered around a specific event, my overdose, and the reasons for it and my inability to address the underlying problems. Certainly, my parents had a hand in all of it. But make no mistake, they were great parents. They loved us with all completely and wanted what was best. They just sometimes got confused about that because of their own fears.

At some point, I needed to be honest with myself and own my shit. I was 29, I had made absolutely the wrong career choice, I didn't know what I would do in the future, and I didn't understand that everything really would be okay.

As an adult, you must take ownership of your circumstances. That doesn't mean I wasn't angry. I was. I wanted my parents to stop trying to fix the problem and offering unsolicited advice.

That mic drop moment was a game changer for me. I had to be honest with them about my feelings in a new way and just hope they understood. At that point they stopped asking me about my career. At that point I became an adult.

And then I excelled.

**"If you laugh, you think, and you cry, that's a full day.
That's a heck of a day. You do that seven days a week,
you're going to have something special."**

-Coach Jim Valvano

I have struggled with stress much of my life, particularly in the morning when I first wake up and my defenses are down. To adjust for that, I've developed my own process to immediately address and reduce my anxiety. The process is not always the same. There are several different actions I may take depending on my time and how I feel.

In this chapter I share them in no particular order.

As you go through this list, remember there are no rules. When doing something becomes a burden, change it up. The idea is to keep your mindset in gratitude and thankfulness, not to be annoying.

1) **Surrender**

You cannot deny your stress or anxiety, but you can surrender it to whoever/whatever you choose.

When I first started, this was a conscious effort. I was taught to say something akin to, "Thank you god for this thought. I surrender it now to the universe and allow it to drift away." I agree that might sound like esoteric, touchy-feely, granola-eating crap. It did to me, but it also worked because it gave me an anchor and I believed it could work.

The idea merely is to acknowledge the stressor and dismiss it instead of providing it energy.

2) **Gratitude Journal**

Surrendering thoughts can be difficult if there is nothing to take their place. You can crowd out the negative with positive thoughts by writing them down.

When you focus on things for which you are grateful it becomes difficult to think about the negatives.

Keeping a journal is not complicated. They actually sell tons of them online. There are all kinds. The particular one I use allows provides space for the following,,,

In the morning:

- Three things for which I am grateful
- Three things that would make that day great

In the evening:

- Three things that went well
- Three things that could have been better (always room for improvement)

While not complicated, keeping a journal can be a pain in the ass. After a week, it may become a challenge. The key, I think, is knowing that the things you list need not be extraordinary. You can be grateful for a sunny day, for your spouse, for rain when the lawn is dry or for a warm coat when it's cold. The idea is that you are replacing negative energy with positive energy.

3) Practice Gratitude, Love and Humility Daily

Uncovering happiness is all about mindset. For me, mindset means actively trying (and often failing) to be a better person every single day. To do that I try to show gratitude for those who have provided me kindness. I tell people I love them, and I own my shit. Boiled down, every day, whenever possible, I try to say:

- Thank you (every day)
- I love you (every day)
- I am sorry (when I screw up)

The key to this is that you use it both with others and with yourself. Forgiving ourselves our transgressions is as important as forgiving others because we are often hardest on ourselves.

4) Send Random Messages of Gratitude and Love

Many mornings, especially on my early morning commute, I'll think about who I know that might be experiencing hardship and whom I love. Then I'll send them a brief text or an email. Sometimes I'll just send a smiley face or a thumbs up with a few words.

When all else fails, I send poo.

These random messages not only pick up the spirits of the unsuspecting recipient, but it always makes me feel good to send them. I just let people know I'm thinking about them and that I care.

This simple act uncovers happiness — both mine and theirs. I'm surprised how often people reply, "Thank you. I needed that." The truth is, I needed that, as well.

We all need a little thank you and love.

And poo.

5) Thank You Notes

Imagine walking to the mailbox and finding a handwritten note thanking you for just being you. What could be more delightful than someone expressing gratitude for having you in their life?

My business partner and close friend Britt Szostak shared this valuable idea. Every day or week or month, whatever works, he sends thank you notes. Sometimes it is to family, friends, or clients. It could be thanking someone for friendship, telling them you admire them, or anything at all.

It makes you feel great for doing it, it makes the recipient feel great and they never forget it. I actually wrote one to myself once and still carry it with me for moments when I'm not feeling good about myself.

6) 365 Days of Gratitude

Karin, my kids, and I keep a family Facebook page to which only we have access. We occasionally use it for silly shit we may find online and the occasional picture.

In 2018, I decided it would be interesting to find something to be grateful for every single day of the year and post it to the page. My thought was that it would move me into gratitude each day, as well as maybe doing the same for the family.

I did it for the entirety of the year. There were certainly times it was helpful and others when it was a pain in the ass. I tried again in 2019 but was not as successful. Now, I use it only when I have something truly significant for which to be thankful.

Again, these things should not be a burden. They are simply different options to try.

7) Read

There are so many insightful books that have opened up my thinking. A few of my favorites have been: *The Power of*

Now by Eckhardt Tolle, *The Art of Happiness* by the Dalai Llama, *The Seven Spiritual Laws of Success* by Deepak Chopra, *The Happiness Advantage* by Shawn Anchor and *10% Happier* by Dan Harris.

On my friends' birthdays, I often send them one of these books as a gift. It is always interesting to see who reads them and what impact it has on them. I am frequently surprised by who tells me they were having a tough time and the book lifted them up.

8) Exercise

We have heard countless times that working out releases endorphins in the brain. All I can tell you is that two years ago I began working out every day and it has changed my psyche. Forget about the physical side — psychologically I am far calmer and more focused after the gym.

Exercise takes you out of that stressful moment. I know that when I am skiing or playing basketball, I am focused only on those moments. Exercise immediately takes me out of my stress.

Enough said.

9) Meditate

I am definitely not an expert here. Much has been written and discussed recently on the topic of meditation, so you don't need me waxing philosophic on the subject.

10% Happier is a great book on the power of meditation. It is written by Dan Harris, a television news correspondent who was a nonbeliever. His journey of transformation was funny and inspiring without being too "out there." He is now a huge proponent and advocate for meditation.

In my experience, taking time out of your day to relax your mind, breath and simply exist has a calming effect.

Follow Your Passion

Beginning in grade school and thereafter, I loved singing. I sang whenever I had the chance, both in school shows and with a variety of bands, the names of which were often more entertaining than the bands, including:

Battle of the Bands, Singing with Unknown Substance.
December 1983. Senior Year of High School. New City, New York

Unknown Substance, 2 Hours Late, The Difference, Mixed Vegetables, The Unforgiven, Banned, and most recently, Bad Art.

When I graduated college, I wanted to sing with a band, but instead I took the detour to law school. I had been performing my entire life, and then as the real world took over, I stopped singing to focus on other pursuits.

Playing Party in the Park with The Difference. Dancing with Mom and Dad. Senior year of college, May 1988. Albany, New York

Not having that outlet in my life left an enormous void. And as much as I had a wonderful and fulfilling life, that creative part of me was still there and I allowed it to be silenced. It was covering up my happiness.

Then my own little miracle happened. In 2005, a variety of unrelated circumstances connected me with five other like-minded local dads who shared my passion for music.

We got together on a few occasions to jam and decided to put our own cover rock band together for fun. We couldn't agree on a name (I thought Love Handles would have been great) so we started out as just Banned. Banned played its first gig in September 2005 at a party in my backyard.

Ultimately, we rebranded ourselves as BAD ART (which were the first initials of everyone in the band at that time– **B**ruce **A**ndy **D**oug **A**nthony **R**ob **T**ony) and have been playing at local events and bars now for 14 years. We have raised close to $100,000 for local charities and have developed a mini local following. It has been a highlight of my life.

Bad Art*

(Pictured Left to right) Anthony Giaccio, Doug Hornyak, me, Andy Wise. Bruce Danziger and Tony Michelini.*Not pictured, original bassist Doug Toback and current drummer Pat Murray

It is also something I have been able to share with my family. All three of our children are accomplished singers and have all lowered their standards and performed with me.

Pam and me singing at my 50th birthday party with George watching. Not pictured is Molly, who also sang with me and is pissed I didn't include a picture with her.

The challenge with taking time and/or money to pursue a passion or an interest is that those things seem the easiest to put off because they seem the least important.

I need to earn a living or *there's no time* or *I'm busy raising my kids* are the usual defaults.

With folks like me, where we are constantly racked with guilt and anxiety, we convince ourselves that if "I take my eye off the ball" for even a second, it will "all fall apart."

To all of the above, I say, "Bullshit, bullshit and more bullshit." Do you really believe we were all put on this earth to simply procreate and then suffer while raising a family just so they can do the same thing? If so, you really need to think it through.

This Book

You think my most recent passion, writing this fucking book, was easy? I have been talking about it but not finishing it for almost ten years. But it was important to me.

I've always wanted to write about my experience and pursue public speaking, an area where I believe I would excel. The process and time commitment at times have been excruciating. Finishing it and seeing where it takes me has had a tremendously positive effect in my happiness.

The older I get, the more I understand that life is short. To give ourselves up to the stress of work without pursuing the things that interest us is to waste our lives.

ROBERT SEGALL, JD

Chapter 25: In Closing

**"Folks are usually about as happy
as they make up their minds to be."**

-Abraham Lincoln

There is so much information out there about happiness and things related to happiness. We ponder the pursuit of happiness, the art of happiness, the secret of happiness. We consider being *present* and finding *the answer* as we meditate, breathe, eat, love, and pray.

There are countless websites, articles, podcasts, YouTube videos and books addressing happiness. Many are written by famous or infamous self-help gurus. Others are written by psychologists or life coaches who feel they have things figured out.

All of them are right on point and all of them completely miss the point.

Human beings are all wired differently. Karin, for example, is far more pragmatic than I am. She simply does not require the help of nor necessarily believes that much of what I written works...*for her*. She absolutely believes it works for me.

Which is the point.   I pieced together a variety of approaches and methods to uncover my happiness.   That works for me. Everyone is different. You are not me (and I am guessing you do not want to be), so your methodology will be different.

Where we probably are similar is that like most people, I am living in the trenches of life every day. I am married with kids. I get up early and go to work. I try to exercise. I want to lose weight. I coach sports. I play softball. I have seemingly never-ending bills that keep increasing. I have unreasonable demands on my time. In other words, I am like you. I am often exhausted. With all of those things, which probably sound much like your life, I finally figured out happiness ... today. Tomorrow it will be a different approach.

I believe most people are like me. They chase happiness every day, but they have no idea what they are looking for. If you found the ideas in this book useful, keep reading the last few paragraphs. If not, throw the book away.

If I were summarizing this book, the key concepts for me in uncovering happiness are the following:

1) Trust yourself (a.k.a. think for yourself).

2) Don't be afraid to follow your passions.

3) Don't be afraid to fail. Tomorrow is another day.

4) Choose your words and actions wisely. People listen and are affected by how we express ourselves far more than you may believe.

5) Stay unattached.

6) Live abundantly.

7) Sometimes love from a distance.

8) Think about what happiness means to you so you'll know what you are looking for.

9) Clean your belly button occasionally. You'd be shocked by what it can smell like in there.

Thank you for taking time out of your day to read this book. Knowing you did lifts my spirit. I hope it made you happy.

Acknowledgements

I wish I could call this book a labor of love. I cannot. It was something I felt I had to complete. It ended up being a labor of necessity. At times I ignored it because it felt like a chore. Other times I discussed it incessantly, to the point where my family and the closest friends with whom I discussed it were understandably annoyed by me. To all of you, I say "thank you" for your patience.

There are many people in my life who had faith in me and have been happy for any success I've experienced. As I try to live in gratitude, there is a good chance that at some point I thanked you and acknowledged your importance in my life. If I have not yet, it is coming! I spend time every day thinking about the people I love and expressing it to them directly. That is part of living in gratitude.

If I do not thank you directly here, please know that it is only because I didn't want to pay for the extra printing. Otherwise you definitely would have made it into the book.

Karin, Pam, Molly and George. You knew I would complete it -- you just didn't know when. I won't speak at length about how much I love you because the book makes it clear. I will just say that you are my entire world. You make me feel like the luckiest son of a bitch on the planet.

Mommy, I know this book may be a little difficult to read at times, but I hope you know how much I love you and Dad. As I say in the book, the same people who pushed me too hard out of

231

love also gave me the strength to complete this book. Furthermore, even though I told you I was a bit hard on Dad in the book, you insisted I finish it.

Britt Szostak, my business partner and close friend. For twenty-three years you have been the voice of reason when I needed to be lifted up, and for the last eight you never let me forget about the book.

Jim Lyman, you read an earlier version and told me to cut the shit and be myself. I needed to hear that.

Andy Laub, Marc and Pattie Lublin, Marc Koerner, Dave Hargraves, Fred Gaston, Rick Van, Steve Older and Nancy Jackson, you never missed an opportunity to ask me when you would get to read the book. I know there are many others as well and every single time I was asked it acted as motivation to finish.

To my mentor, Steve D'Annunzio. Thank you for your guidance and helping me through some tough spots in my life. More recently, thank you for seeking me out years after we stopped working together to remind me to complete this book and help me chart a course.

Nicole Brandon. Your insights into what I was trying to say and adding structure allowed me to refocus on what I needed the book to be.

Steve Harbaugh, my coach. Thank you for keeping me focused these last four years and gently pointing me in the right direction.

David Klinghoffer. Thank you for that thorough finalread-through.

I have several essential non-book acknowledgements.

Steve Segall. I am so impressed and proud of you. Change comes from within and that makes you a big success.

Mo Segall. Thank you for being present in the times I needed you.

Doug Toback. Knowing I have a friend who is sincerely happy for me when things go well and who has been there when they do not is a blessing.

Polly Condit. You found ways to help me understand who I was and who I am. Thank you from the bottom of my heart.

Greg Large. You have always provided support and friendship.

Larry Greenberg and Andy Laub. The kindness and compassion you showed me early in my career will never be forgotten. Thank you for always being my biggest supporter.

The Potluck Boys. Kenny Regan, Jeff Klarsfeld, Adam Zahl and Eric Koss. To have lifelong friends who are all still close is the greatest blessing. I love you guys.

Tony Michelini, Anthony Giaccio, Doug Hornyak, Brice Danziger, Andy Wise, Pat Murray and Doug Toback — my bandmates — thank you for allowing me to keep music in my life.

Finally, thank you to anyone taking the time to read this. It means the world to me.

Love,

Rob

R ob Segall was birthed by a midwife on a farm in Arkansas in 1966. After winning the Heisman Trophy as a college quarterback, Rob decided to forgo the NFL and instead focus on his first passion: Law.

All bullshit aside, Rob graduated Brooklyn Law School in 1991 and four and half years later tried to kill himself.

The good news is that with the love support of his high school sweetheart, Karin, an accomplished lawyer, wife and super mom, Rob launched a career in financial services and financial planning that ended up going a lot better better than he expected. The best part of Rob's job is that he loves his clients, many of whom have become close friends. Whether any of them love him back is another story.

Rob and Karin live in Westchester County, a suburb of New York City and have three incredible children, Pam, Molly and George and their dogs, Walter and Reggie.

Rob Segall works as a financial planner in New York City, where he has a wonderful career as a Managing Director at Lenox Advisors.

In his spare time, Rob is active local volunteer, amateur musician and mediocre softball player.

Made in the USA
Middletown, DE
19 November 2020